THE
SERVANT
PRINCIPLE

THE
FINDING FULFILLMENT
SERVANT
THROUGH OBEDIENCE TO CHRIST
PRINCIPLE

RICK E. FERGUSON
WITH
BRYAN MCANALLY

BROADMAN
& HOLMAN
PUBLISHERS

Nashville, Tennessee

0–8054–1821–0

Published by Broadman & Holman Publishers, Nashville, Tennessee
Acquisitions and Development Editor: Leonard G. Goss
Pages Design and Typesetting: TF Designs, Mt. Juliet, Tennessee

Dewey Decimal Classification: 248
Subject Heading: CHRISTIAN SERVICE
Library of Congress Card Catalog Number: 98–53136

Unless otherwise noted, Scripture quotations are from the Holy Bible,
New International Version, © copyright 1973, 1978, 1984 by
International Bible Society.

Library of Congress Cataloging-in-Publication Data

Ferguson, Rick E., 1956–
    The servant principle: fulfilling your God-designed destiny / by
Rick E. Ferguson.
        p. cm.
    Includes bibliographical references.
    ISBN 0–8054–1821–0
    1. Service (Theology) 1. Title.
BT738.4.F47 1999
248—dc21   98–53136
                                                                    CIP

2 3 4 5 03

In dedication to
my parents,
Rev. W. E. and Valene Ferguson,
who have modeled the Servant Principle
all their lives.

Contents

༄༅༅

Part Three:
Servants, Not Celebrities

Part Four:
The Principal Servant

Part Five:
The Suffering Servant

Part Six:
The Servant Evangelist

Part Seven:
The Servant Leader

Part Eight:
The Servant and the New World Order

Acknowledgments

The Servant Principle has been a cooperative effort and labor of love in which many people invested. Thank you, Bryan McAnally, for contributing your superb writing and editing skills in moving the Servant Principle from sermon series to book. Also, thank you Jo Loftis for contributing your skilled editorial eyes to the final manuscripts.

The Servant Principle would not have been written were it not for the encouragement, support, and help of Drew Stephens, director of Hope for Today Ministries and the faithful board members of Hope for Today. A special thanks goes to my administrative assistant, Susan Robinson, who has helped to manage and supervise the progress of this project.

Also, I express my deep, abiding love and appreciation for the Riverside Baptist Church family. Thank you for being receptive and responsive to our weekly ministry of the Word of God. Thank you for your continual encouragement and prayer support. Thank you for granting me the holy honor of being your pastor.

Finally, I thank my wonderful wife, Kathy, and our three incredible kids: Brett, Katie, and Justin. Thanks for your patience with me, your suggestions along the way, and for bringing daily joy, laughter, and strength to my life.

Part One:

The Servant Principle

Chapter 1

Life with Purpose

~~~

Only seven days separated the deaths of two women known best by their first names. When each died, the world wept. Though grief, shock, and tears were common commodities shared by the entire world, the lives of Princess Diana and Mother Teresa stand in stark contrast.

Their lives represented both ends of many spectrums. One had an empire's wealth at her disposal; the other had no possessions of her own. One traveled daily among the world's sick and hurting and impoverished; the other was the headliner at the affairs of the rich and famous. One had a life of inner turmoil; the other possessed peace passing all understanding. One continually sought purpose and meaning; the other demonstrated those findings daily. One spent her life being served; the other spent her life serving others. One was a princess in worldly kingdoms; the other was a servant in the kingdom of God.

Many women envied Diana's lifestyle—the opulence, power, comfort, and opportunities she enjoyed. We couldn't make sense of the news that she never found joy, satisfaction, peace, and purpose in that lifestyle. She had the world in her palms, yet happiness and meaning slipped through her fingers.

At the same time, few of us would have chosen the life of Mother Teresa—the sacrifice, the intense labor, the thankless reward, hardship, and loneliness. But few would argue that this woman's life contained more purpose and meaning, more personal peace and satisfaction than did Diana's. Mother Teresa was a servant to the forgotten people of the world. She demonstrated that servanthood is more than a lifestyle. It is simply a life.

The life of a servant.

Servanthood. It is not a very popular subject. Servanthood has a cost of personal investment that goes against everything we are taught. Servanthood totally conflicts with the self-centeredness ingrained in every person. The thought of becoming a servant is completely repulsive. The request to deny all personal desires is never met with excitement. No one wants to hear the call to relinquish all personal rights and privileges. No one wants to accept the challenge to develop a slave's mindset. Servanthood contradicts absolutely every single thing inside us. Everything. Everything, that is, except the Spirit of God.

Servant Living = Purposeful Living

God has given every one of us a desire to excel, to feel that life counts for something. Everybody wants to believe life has significance and that each person can make a difference. We all want to be remembered for having a long-term impact on the world. Life's search is one of meaning and purpose. We hope, when we're gone, our having been here would be remembered positively by others. All people desire, to some degree, to do something great with their lives. Every person would like to leave a legacy.

This passion to find real purpose is God-given. No one ever says, "All I want to do with my life is simply occupy space and suck air." All human beings want more than simply to exist. God gives this common desire to excel to all people because he made humans in his own image. Humans are specially created with the same compulsion toward excellence as their Creator. A sense of purpose causes a person to get out of bed every morning, to show up to work on time, to give his or her best effort. It compels a person to volunteer, to give money to the homeless, or to help a neighbor build a fence. A sense of purpose causes new generations to be born, technology to advance, and exploration to continue. A sense of purpose is not a by-product of cosmic chance, of Darwinistic evolution, or of mere fate.

The desire to find life's purpose sets humans apart from animals. Animals don't need a sense of purpose. A full food dish or a pat on the head gives a family pet every bit of meaning it could ever want. A trough of food and a corral for shelter provides a farm animal with all it needs. Animals live exclusively out of a survival instinct; living is their sole purpose. Horses, cows, pigs, dogs—all animals—never exhaust one ounce of mental energy wondering why they are alive or if their lives are making a positive difference in the world.

Humans are different. Humans are not simply a more highly evolved animal. Humans are God's masterpiece. We are his creation's crowning achievement. Every human is purposefully created. Humans are

> ✑
> *God's Word says he uniquely created you in his very image with design and with meaning.*

no product of evolutionary adaptive "survival of the fittest." In fact, evolution demoralizes and dehumanizes humanity. Evolution is detrimental to the human condition because it lies, telling people they exist for no reason other than cosmic chance. Each progressing generation has less scruples, morals, and consciousness than the one before because each has been more convincingly schooled to believe nothing in life has meaning or purpose. They have been duped to think they are merely a coincidence of nature.

God says something far more dignifying about his people than what our world's educational systems offer. God provides an explanation for life that is highlighted by a sense of purpose. God's Word says he uniquely created you in his very image with design and with meaning. God placed something inside of you that will not let you settle for an atheistic, dehumanizing, evolutionary analysis of your life. Mixing Christianity and evolution is like trying to mix oil and water. The two are diametrically opposed. Your life is a gift from God. As such, your life has purpose.

God wants you to find the true purpose of your life. Suddenly, the road before you forks, and you will be faced with choices, challenges, and life-changing decisions.

Soon you will see the life to which God calls his followers. You will see his call on you. He will show you opportunities to serve him every day in every way. He will show you the servant he was and continues to be. He will show you the Servant Principle.

Chapter 2

Falling from the Ladder

∽∽∽

The ladder of success rises high, but nobody seems to be standing on the same rung. The average person reports to work and sees exactly where she is positioned on the ladder. The woman in the neighboring office has more seniority. The man working on her other side, though less tenured, receives a higher salary. The new hire, though younger and fresh out of college, is suddenly her boss. Indeed, the reality of today makes the statement "all people are created equal" an outdated phrase.

Whether male or female, you may feel just like this woman. Sometimes you may wonder if anyone at all is looking up from the rung beneath your feet. Climbing the ladder of success can be frustrating. You may invest years trying to climb a single level. When you finally step up, you may discover the benefits aren't what you imagined them to be. Moreover, you may have little guarantee your position on the higher rung is secure. This is the age of downsizing and corporate reorganization. The decision of one leader, looking at the bottom financial line, may return you to the bottom rung, which leaves you doubting you can ever climb as high as you originally aspired.

The truth is, the ladder of success is as old as it is tall. People have been looking up and plotting their next advance since the cockcrow of humanity. The ladder of success has always been around. Solomon rose high on the ladder with unmatched riches and seven hundred wives. Before him, King David looked down the ladder and, seeing Bathsheba, kicked her husband Uriah off the ladder to his death so she could be queen. Long before David, countless notables scaled the ladder by squirming under others, squeezing around them, or shoving them out of the way.

The ladder, just by its existence, is not evil. The ladder of success is simply an outgrowth of the God-given passion for purpose. Humanity's sinful nature makes climbing the ladder an evil, treacherous adventure. The Bible records both the origin of the ladder and the sinful allure of getting to the utmost rung. Cain, the first child of Adam and Eve, clawed his way over his brother, Abel, in an act of jealous, murdering rage. Cain possessed a flawed understanding of what it took to be the best, standing atop the ladder's upper rungs. His misunderstanding was sinful, deadly, and life-corrupting.

Humankind's approach to finding success changed perspective in the Garden of Eden before Cain and Abel were even born. Originally, Adam and Eve's sense of purpose and sense of identity were wrapped exclusively in their relationship with God. They possessed no need for a ladder because success was obtained simply by their being in relationship with God. After the fall in the Garden of Eden, man's sense of purpose became man's search for purpose. The ladder was created as a tool to get above it all, to aid the search, to gain a proper perspective. Ironically, the higher the climb on the ladder, it seems, the more skewed the perspective becomes. No longer is a person's search for purpose wrapped up in God. It is wrapped up in self. We have made the terrible shift from God-centered living to self-centered living. Now it has become more important to climb higher on the ladder than to obtain the proper perspective of a successful, purpose-filled life.

Our search for purpose moved from relational identities to life's activities. That shift took place long before you or I were born. As descendants of Adam and Eve, the shift was born in us all, eternally altering our search for purpose and identity. Sin distorted our legitimate God-given need to sense we are making an impact in the world. That distortion corrupts both why we climb the ladder of success and everything we do in an attempt to reach the next rung.

The results of the fall have been devastating and deadly. People now struggle to find purpose and meaning in what they do rather than in who they are. Selfish ambition has replaced our search for purpose. This distortion has blinded people to Jesus. He revealed the true key for discovering genuine greatness, meaning, purpose,

> �
> *People now struggle to find purpose and meaning in what they do rather than in who they are.*

and significance in life. When Jesus tried to tell his people, it sounded confusing. It sounded like a paradox, an oxymoron. It sounded like a contradiction in terms. Jesus said:

- The only way you can find true life is to lose your life.
- The only way to be first is to be willing to be last.

These paradoxical truths formulate the Servant Principle.

Jesus embodied the Servant Principle. He designed the servant's job for each of his followers, and he was the first to perfectly fill that position. He said he came not to be served, but to serve. Jesus himself modeled the servant life. Philippians 2:1–11 explicitly details the lifestyle governed by the Servant Principle:

> If you have any encouragement from being united with Christ, if any comfort from his love, if any fellowship with the Spirit, if any tenderness and compassion, then make my joy complete by being like-minded, having the same love, being one in spirit and purpose. Do nothing out of selfish ambition or vain conceit, but in humility consider others better than yourselves. Each of you should look not only to your own interests, but also to the interests of others.

Your attitude should be the same as that of Christ Jesus:

Who, being in very nature God,
did not consider equality with God something to be
grasped,
but made himself nothing,
taking the very nature of a servant,
being made in human likeness.
And being found in appearance as a man,
he humbled himself
and became obedient to death—
even death on a cross!
Therefore God exalted him to the highest place
and gave him the name that is above every name,
that at the name of Jesus every knee should bow,
in heaven and on earth and under the earth,
and every tongue confess that Jesus Christ is Lord,
to the glory of God the Father.

Jesus was the originator and example of servanthood, and he is reproducing his life of selfless service in people today. Jesus Christ understood the link between servanthood and a purposeful life. He places his invitation to servanthood at the feet of his disciples, wanting all to follow his example of servanthood.

Think back a moment. Who was the greatest person who ever lived? Without question, no person more greatly impacted the course of history than Jesus Christ. He didn't do it through wars, conquest, and domination. His life was that of a servant. He changed the world by devoting his life to serving his fellow man and woman.

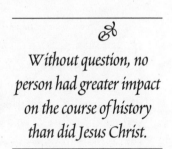

Without question, no person had greater impact on the course of history than did Jesus Christ.

"The way to become great," Jesus said, "is to become a servant." Doesn't that sound crazy? Jesus introduced his disciples to the Servant

Principle when they all were jockeying for position and prestige. All twelve wanted to move up the corporate ladder of their day. They were searching for purpose in life by trying to become power brokers. They all wanted to have power and control. Jesus told them if they were looking for their lives' real meaning, they had leaned their ladders against the wrong wall. He told them that real purpose would not be found in self-promotion, but instead in slavery:

> Then the mother of Zebedee's sons came to Jesus with her sons and, kneeling down, asked a favor of him.
>
> "What is it you want?" he asked.
>
> She said, "Grant that one of these two sons of mine may sit at your right and the other at your left in your kingdom."
>
> "You don't know what you are asking," Jesus said to them. "Can you drink the cup I am going to drink?"
>
> "We can," they answered.
>
> Jesus said to them, "You will indeed drink from my cup, but to sit at my right or left is not for me to grant. These places belong to those for whom they have been prepared by my Father."
>
> When the ten heard about this, they were indignant with the two brothers. Jesus called them together and said, "You know that the rulers of the Gentiles lord it over them, and their high officials exercise authority over them. Not so with you. Instead, whoever wants to become great among you must be your servant, and whoever wants to be first must be your slave—just as the Son of Man did not come to be served, but to serve, and to give his life as a ransom for many" (Matt. 20:20–28).

In this passage, Jesus described the thrust of the Servant Principle with two different words. Jesus said greatness comes from being a servant (v. 26). *Servant* comes from the word *diakonos,* from which the word *deacon* is derived. Originally the word meant "kicking up dust." It came to be associated with a servant so anxious to serve, he kicked up dust running to obey his master. The word means a voluntary offer to serve.

Jesus went further, using a word even more emotionally packed than *diakonos*. He used the word *doulas* (v. 27), which is "slave." This person is totally subjugated; physically, emotionally, mentally subservient to another. Literally, this person is a slave. Jesus said if you want to be great, you must have the mind of a servant and the heart of a slave.

Do you really want your life to count? Do you want to find your life's genuine purpose and meaning? Do you want to know what true success is? Do you really want to be and do something great? Push aside the ladder you've been climbing. Look toward your Savior. Jesus gives the key opening the door to a purpose-filled life.

Jesus said the key is becoming a servant!

Chapter 3

Opening the Locks of Life

〜〜〜

The search had begun. The family waited in the car, Bibles in hand. The clock chimed. Fifteen minutes until the start of Sunday school. The iron had been turned off. Mike hustled to the door, instinctively reaching for the wall peg where his car keys would be hanging.

They weren't there.

Time to panic.

He scanned the coffee table by the door, thinking maybe he had dropped the keys there last night. Nothing. He ran to the bedroom, scouring his bureau, nightstand, and bed. Nothing. Mike sprinted to the bathroom, stumbling over a pile of dirty clothes. The counter, shower stall, and toilet tank were all disturbingly car-key free.

Back to the living room, Mike jumped on the couch, pushing cushions haphazardly onto the floor. He thought he heard the sound of keys jingling as he switched hands for the search, so he dug deeper. He looked at the clock. He had seven minutes to get to church. In a final act of desperation, Mike scurried to the garage. Maybe his wife had taken the keys with her to start the car. He stepped to the passenger side of the car and, with a bent wrist and closed fist turning in tiny counter-clockwise circles, made the universal "roll-down-the-window-please" gesture. She complied. Mike asked in a huff, "Have you seen the keys?"

She paused a moment, determining if he was serious. Remembering she married him despite his quirks, she politely spoke. "Dear, they are in your other hand."

Mike looked down. She wasn't lying.

They had been in his hands the entire time. The sound of the keys he thought he had heard while on the couch was indeed the keys. They jingled when he switched them from hand to hand. He was so intent on finding them, he never bothered to look in his own palm.

This common story has probably happened to someone you know. Maybe your mother forgot she placed her eyeglasses atop her head and spent the next twenty minutes squinting for them in a fruitless quest. Maybe your husband searched for the ringing cordless telephone stuffed in his back pocket. "I know it's here somewhere," he said, turning frustrated circles, hoping to locate it before the caller disconnected. Something like this may have happened to you. Whatever the situation, the lost item was either literally or figuratively right under your nose, yet the thought to look in the most obvious place never arose.

The search for life's keys is a similar quest. Our most often asked question is "Why am I here?" or some variation of it. Life is a locked vault; most people spend life searching without success for the keys to unlock the answers that lie hidden deep within.

God, in his love, constantly reminds us that the keys he smiths for life's locks lie within our hands. He doesn't hide anything from us. He simply waits for us to realize we have the key. Jesus Christ is the key to the locks in our lives.

Jesus understood life's quest. When all the disciples tried different keys of power, persuasion, and authority to provide their life with meaning, Jesus simply offered the one key providing real meaning. Jesus showed that committing life to servanthood was the key to life's questions and searches.

~

To Be Truly Great

Jesus knew and showed that servanthood is the key to attaining true greatness. True greatness is not accumulated by power associated with position. Human achievement cannot acquire it. "Whoever wants to become great among you must be your servant" (Matt. 20:26). True greatness is attained only by sacrifice, humility, surrender, obedience, and total dependence upon Jesus Christ.

Judgment day will likely hold a lot of surprises. Many of the world's "A-list" people, once considered great, will find themselves without an invitation to the recognition party. Many Christian celebrities will be last to be applauded in eternity. Conversely, many of the so-called "nameless nobodies" who gave their lives in humble service without applause or recognition will be first. God will recognize them for their greatness.

> *True greatness is attained only by sacrifice, humility, surrender, obedience, and total dependence upon Jesus Christ.*

What dictates our measure of greatness? Is the preacher who stands before crowds and cameras every Sunday greater than the people volunteering their time changing dirty diapers and wiping runny noses in the nursery? Often, the unseen, everyday work of unknown servants surpasses the efforts of clergy. Even Christians continue to measure greatness by the same false, superficial standards the world uses—fame and fortune.

The church body itself can buy into a worldly standard of success, monitoring progress by buildings, bodies, and budgets. Every sin an individual can commit, the church corporate body can commit. The church's and a Christian's true greatness is measured only by faithfulness and love for Jesus. Nothing more. Actually, true greatness may cost buildings, bodies, and budgets.

~

Can You Relate?

Jesus knew and showed that becoming a servant is the key to strong personal relationships. This is the secret to getting along with people—even unreasonable, unlovable types of people. If you want to get along with others, quit trying to change them. Instead, look at changing yourself. Take the attitude of a servant. Every single personal conflict is ultimately rooted in self-centeredness and selfishness.

Think how married couples could benefit if husband and wife refrained from being selfish. Each should stop threatening the other with divorce if individual needs are not met. Every good marriage needs one wedding and two funerals. For this to happen, we should all work hard to please our spouses first and ourselves last.

Think about how much happier communities would be if everyone quit trying to protect his own turf. Instead, people should humble themselves and extend a helping, uplifting hand to those who live around them.

Even churches striving for perfection need to understand servanthood. Think about how much more could be accomplished if everyone quit jockeying for position. Imagine if we all stopped trying to get our own way. A radical revolution would take place if we really started preferring the needs of others above our own, putting others first and humbly serving. If all people would have the same humble servant attitude of Christ Jesus, existing broken human relationships would be fixed.

~

Live Life to the Fullest

Jesus knew and showed that servanthood is the key to discovering spiritual life. Jesus taught that the only way to have real life is to die to self. The only way to live in close relationship with him is to obey him as a servant:

I tell you the truth, unless a kernel of wheat falls to the ground and dies, it remains only a single seed. But if it dies, it produces many seeds. The man who loves his life will lose it, while the man who hates his life in this world will keep it for eternal life. Whoever serves me must follow me; and where I am, my servant also will be. My Father will honor the one who serves me (John 12:24–26).

Most Christians never experience the fullness of life rightfully theirs in Christ because they never fully understand the crucified life. Most Christians understand the crucified life theoretically, not experientially. Jesus said, "If any man will come after me, let him deny himself, and take up his cross daily, and follow me" (Luke 9:23 KJV). To know him and to live in constant fellowship with him means to die to everything we call our own.

The apostle Paul discovered this concept:

But whatever was to my profit I now consider loss for the sake of Christ. What is more, I consider everything a loss compared to the surpassing greatness of knowing Christ Jesus my Lord, for whose sake I have lost all things. I consider them rubbish, that I may gain Christ (Phil. 3:7–8).

Most Christians never experience the crucified life because they are too concerned with holding on to what is theirs.

~

Lean on Me

Jesus knew and showed that the key to a fulfilling life of obedience and dependence comes through servanthood. A servant is obedient to his master. Jesus modeled this concept when "he humbled himself and became obedient to death—even death on a cross!" (Phil. 2:8). Serving Jesus Christ means living in unreserved obedience to him. In the servant's heart, two particular words never go together. Those words are, "no, Lord." A servant is always obedient.

A servant is also dependent on his master. Slavery means not only to make oneself subservient to another but also to place oneself in a position of total dependence upon another. It means to be in bondage to another. The Bible says Jesus became a servant, living in total dependence upon the Father. In the Incarnation, Jesus will-ingly surrendered his rights as coregent with the Father to assume the humble position of codependence upon the Father.

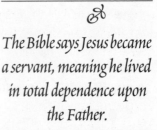

The Bible says Jesus became a servant, meaning he lived in total dependence upon the Father.

"Jesus gave them this answer: 'I tell you the truth, the Son can do noth-ing by himself; he can do only what he sees his Father doing, because what-ever the Father does the Son also does'" (John 5:19). If Jesus could do nothing by himself, what would make us think we can do anything by our-selves? We are powerless. When we oppose God's control, we pave our path to failure. God is in control.

He is your King. Let him rule.

Get off the throne of your life.

Let Jesus, the appropriate King, sit in his seat. The life of a true servant is one of total dependence. A well-developed servant's heart abandons the life of self-sufficiency and assumes the life of total dependence upon Jesus Christ. The challenge is to adopt the attitude of a servant. By doing so, a servant develops the attitude of Jesus Christ himself.

Be Like Christ

Jesus knew and showed that becoming a servant is the key to overcom-ing human nature's resistance to God's will. Human nature keeps us from signing on as a "slave of righteousness." No one really wants to do the sub-servient, menial, behind the scenes tasks, the "grunt work." Most people prefer tasks and positions placing them in the spotlight, drawing human recognition and applause. No one really wants to prefer other people's needs above their own individual needs. No one really wants to get into the business of "washing dirty feet."

No one really wants to give up everything, abandon all claims to ownership and personal rights. Everyone would much prefer to speak up rather than shut up.

People are this way because of human nature. We are inherently selfish and not servant-minded. Servanthood does not come naturally. It only comes supernaturally. In the fall in the garden of Eden, we moved from God-centered living to self-centered living. The whole goal of God in Jesus Christ's redemption was to return us back to God-centered living. Christ came as a servant to demonstrate God-centered living for all humankind.

Servants don't have to set out on their own, searching for answers. Servants don't have to rely upon their own insufficient wit, guile, or talent. God shows his servants the way to live life. He shows his purpose for a servant's existence.

Total obedience.

Total dependence.

This is what it means to be a servant of Jesus Christ.

Chapter 4

A Measure of Greatness

~~~

In our day, servanthood has become a forgotten art. According to the world's thinking, the entire concept is tired, worn-out. Some people still hire maids to clean their homes or cook meals. Many wealthy families still employ nannies to provide care for the children they are too busy to care for themselves. Make no mistake, though, the true servant in today's world is nearly extinct. Maids and nannies today are well compensated for their jobs. Their jobs are a service, and they are paid handsomely. But take away their paycheck, and their loyalty will stray. Few people are willing to do that type of work simply because they love serving others. Today's world has few servants because everybody is fighting so hard to be the person at the top of the pile. Everybody wants a servant, but nobody is willing to be one.

Jesus Christ is calling for servants. The world doesn't reward the servanthood he wants us to perform. We will see no paycheck. We won't receive health or retirement benefits. Retirement is not even allowed. We won't receive perks like a company car, tuition reimbursement, or free room and board. "Vacation" is merely a euphemism for "mission trip." We won't even be given the assurance we will be able to work in a safe environment.

In another sense, the job to which God calls us does offer the best benefits. God offers us fringe benefits the world could never understand or match. While the world sees us struggling, we can take rest and comfort in God's presence. When the world sees us serving in areas where progress is invisible and unlikely, we can voice our concerns and needs directly to God in prayer. When the world backs away in fear as we serve in harrowing locations and situations, we can continue confidently with the knowledge that we perform safely by being in the center of God's will. The benefits are amazing and exceed everything the world can offer.

Daily Tests and Challenges

Despite the Holy Spirit's pull to follow God, fleshly instincts urge us to flee. The selfish disposition we were born with is our nature. It fights and resists any attempt to becoming a servant. This is why people need to be born again. In the new birth, Jesus imparts his divine nature to us. When a person has truly been spiritually reborn, the Holy Spirit inside compels that person to constantly move from self-centered living to God-centered living. As a Christian, be forewarned: the internal battle will be great when you begin to take on the heart and ministry of a servant. Here are examples of where you will be tested in the flesh:

> *When you have been truly born again, something inside you compels you to constantly move from self-centered living to God-centered living.*

- When someone insults you—servants turn the other cheek, returning blessing for cursing. The flesh, on the other hand, mounts a counterattack, always fighting back.
- When someone asks you to give of your time, talents, or treasure—

servants give everything possible, even walking the extra mile if necessary. The flesh grasps, protects, and clings onto personal time and schedules.

* When you face suffering and pain—servants face hardship, suffering, and injustice with quiet confidence and continual joy. The flesh gripes, complains, and questions God.

* When you serve or perform tasks faithfully—servants expect no recognition or reward. The flesh desires self-glory or applause, always wanting compensation and recognition.

* When you don't get your way and face disappointment—servants continue to praise God, content in every situation. The flesh is never content or satisfied, always wanting more.

* When asked to sacrifice your own preferences for the sake of others—servants never demand their own way or preferences but gladly sacrifice them for others. The flesh constantly demands to have things its own way.

* When asked to do menial tasks—servants see no task as too menial or humble. Servants never feel too good to wash dirty feet. The flesh wants no part in dirty, humbling, menial tasks. It wants power, position, and prestige.

* When asked to serve—servants gladly respond and serve to fulfill a purpose in life. The flesh does not want to serve, but instead wants to be served.

* When you see sin in other people—servants grieve over sin in people's lives and have compassion and mercy toward them. The flesh responds with "self-righteous indignation," criticism, judgment, and condemnation.

* When you see someone who is "down and out"—servants respond with love, mercy, generosity, and acceptance. Servants tend to the wounded person on the side of the road, covering wounds and helping him to his feet. The flesh snubs its nose and passes the wounded, too concerned with its own agenda to make time for those really hurting.

* When as8ked to follow someone else's leadership—servants gladly follow spiritual leaders with a spirit of love and joy, constantly

encouraging those who lead. The flesh resists following anyone. It is constantly critical, cynical, and suspicious.

- When asked to submit to authority—servants gladly submit to the authorities God places over them. The flesh resists submitting to any authority, saying "No one will rule over me." Servants have a sweet spirit of submission, while the flesh has a bitter spirit of rebellion.
- When asked to step out of your comfort zone—servants gladly vacate comfort zones, understanding that Christ's call is not to a life of comfort and convenience, but to a life of surrender, sacrifice, and sometimes, suffering. The flesh resists abandoning the comfort zone. It wants coddling, never wanting to do anything uncomfortable or inconvenient.
- When asked to forgive someone who has truly offended you—servants gladly and intentionally forgive because they have been forgiven of so much. The flesh refuses to forgive offenders. It feels justified in holding grudges and harboring bitterness and anger.
- When other people receive recognition and reward—servants rejoice with those who rejoice. They find joy in the successes of other people. The flesh feels jealousy and hostility when others succeed.

God knows your selfish flesh resists your developing a servanthood lifestyle and attitude:

> For they that are after the flesh do mind the things of the flesh; but they that are after the Spirit the things of the Spirit. For to be carnally minded is death; but to be spiritually minded is life and peace. Because the carnal mind is enmity against God: for it is not subject to the law of God, neither indeed can be. So then they that are in the flesh cannot please God. But ye are not in the flesh, but in the Spirit, if so be that the Spirit of God dwell in you. Now if any man have not the Spirit of Christ, he is none of his (Rom. 8:5–9 KJV).

You get to choose between two ways of living your life each day. The choice is, Am I going to serve myself or am I going to serve others? The two options are considered a million times in a million different ways. When Christ saved us, he called us to a life of self-abandonment, self-sacrifice, surrender, obedience, dependence, and unreserved service. We are faced with this choice even now. As we look at the job description for servanthood, a simple question sprouts from our brain like an emerging flower from the spring soil: Why should I?

What could motivate you to give up self-centered living and take on the heart and life of a servant?

When Christ saved you, he called you to a life of self-abandonment, self-sacrifice, surrender, obedience, dependence, and unreserved service.

Part Two:

The Call to Serve

Chapter 5

The Incentive Clause

∽∽∽

We live in the age of the superstar athlete. Baseball pitcher Pedro Martinez signed a six-year contract with the Boston Red Sox paying him $12.5 million per year, beginning in 1998. Basketball legend Michael Jordan agreed to play for $33 million in 1997. Football star Steve Young inked a contract that pays him $8 million a year until he retires. On top of salaries, these athletes make millions of dollars through endorsements and movie roles. They make enough money to provide for the next five generations of their family.

The athletes who aren't superstars have to work harder for their money. Without name recognition ensuring their team's financial prosperity, they try to earn extra money by meeting incentives. Incentive clauses are placed in a player's contract, and when the athlete meets or exceeds the incentive criteria, the team pays that player more money.

~

Jesus, Our Motivator

While becoming a servant of Jesus Christ may seem thankless, God does provide great incentives for following his son. These incentives motivate the believer into a daily life of subservience and service for the benefit of God's kingdom. The Holy Spirit offers our motivation:

> If you have any encouragement from being united with Christ,
> if any comfort from his love, if any fellowship with the Spirit,
> if any tenderness and compassion. . . .
> Your attitude should be the same as that of Christ Jesus
> (Phil. 2:1, 5).

The apostle Paul built a case for true humility and servanthood in these verses. He understood that everything within us will fight to skip over Scripture exhorting us to take on Christ's servant attitude. So he reminded us why we should do it. He reminded us of all we have been freely given in Christ Jesus.

~

The Consolation of Christ

Philippians 2:1 reminds us that we have encouragement from being united in Christ. The Greek translation of this word means "to call alongside." This same basic word is used as a title given to the Holy Spirit by Jesus when he said, "And I will ask the Father, and he will give you another Counselor (*parakletes*) to be with you forever" (John 14:16). The word describes someone who comes alongside to help us, to lift us up, to encourage us, or to support and strengthen us. The word is a beautiful description of what it means to be united with Jesus Christ.

Those who have had Jesus Christ walk with them through a tragedy know how his presence sustains a person. The consolation of Jesus Christ has enabled thousands of people throughout the years to make the statement, "I don't know how anyone could face any problem without Jesus."

His constant gift of encouragement is the motive for believers to be humble and broken.

~

The Comfort of Christ's Love

As a pastor, I have performed literally hundreds of funerals. I have officiated ceremonies for the saved and the unsaved. I've presided over funerals for Christian families and for families who have no faith in God. The most noticeable difference between the two types of families I have witnessed is the believers' experience of Christ's love. Their comfort is visible, evident, and undeniable. When the pain of death and separation pierces the heart of the believer, the love of Jesus Christ actively, attentively, and purposefully cushions the sting and begins mending the ragged hole left behind.

This is not to say bereaved Christians do not mourn. Their hearts ache because of the loss. Their tears stream just as heavily as they reflect on happy memories. Their lips quiver and their throats thicken and choke up as they attempt to eulogize their beloved friend or family member. The homes' hallways still echo with laughter of past joys. Favorite chairs remain empty. Pictures are still poignant reminders of the beloved's best qualities. Death is death. Loss is loss, regardless of salvation. It hurts all the same, and when you hurt, you will mourn.

Even though the experience of death is the same for Christians and non-Christians, it is also much different. The unsaved feel helpless while a dying kin or friend struggles for life, but Christians find solace in knowing that everything that occurs does so above the caring net of God's will. The lost search fruitlessly for a purpose in death, but the saved rest in the comfort that all things, even death, serve a definite purpose orchestrated by God. When the unbeliever drops to the bed, burying hot tears in the depth of pillows and shouting blame to God, the believer drops to knees bruised from constant prayer, lifting hands in praise and shouting, "Rejoice that God is still God!" In the bleakest hours, when death is the only certainty, the future is filled with agonizing questions, and when the stark reality of saying your final good-bye coldly slaps a stinging smack across your face, God's love is the only comfort.

And it is sufficient.

You only have to think of your own salvation to remember when you have been comforted by his love. You can likely think of times in your Christian walk when you have been lifted up by the Holy Spirit. The Holy Spirit reminded you that Jesus loves you unconditionally. He loves you at all times, even when you are unloving and unlovable. If you have ever been comforted by his love, then pay it back in servanthood.

Companionship of the Holy Spirit

> *The moment you accepted Christ as your Savior, you received the gift of constant companionship from the Holy Spirit.*

The companionship of the Holy Spirit should compel you to servanthood. The moment you accepted Christ as your Savior, you received the gift of constant companionship from the Holy Spirit. He lives inside you. He is your closest neighbor, your most reliable confidant. When you are defeated, the Holy Spirit is there to remind you of your victory in Christ. When you are sad, the Holy Spirit reminds you of the joy of the Lord. When you are lonely, the Holy Spirit reminds you that Christ will never depart from you. When you are at your end, the Holy Spirit reminds you of your new beginning in Jesus. When you have given up, the Holy Spirit reminds you of your hope in your Savior.

The Holy Spirit came as the seal of your salvation. He is God's earnest guarantee of the completeness and security of your position in Christ. If you want to recognize the fellowship of the Holy Spirit, do it in servanthood.

~

Compassion of the Father

Christians enjoy the Holy Spirit's fellowship because of God's compassion. They have received his grace, mercy, tenderness, forgiveness, and love. All people—saved and unsaved—are benefactors of the Father's compassion. The unsaved experience it every time they utter defiance toward God. They vocally deny God with the mouth God shaped, using the vocal cords he designed, pushing out air he stirs from lungs he created. They think poisonous thoughts, using the mind God built, and are still allowed to continue living because of God's grace. People spend so much time griping about how unfair God is to them that they never look at life through God's eyes. If God used the same concept of fairness ruling the ways of modern humanity, modern humanity would cease to exist! God, though, has grace and compassion, which far exceed human understanding. His compassion alone allows tomorrows to continue coming.

Every person who ever bowed at the cross, saying, "You are Lord, Jesus. Please be my Savior," has received God's undeserved compassion. As a recipient of his compassion, you should not rebel when he asks you to have a servant's gentle, humble, obedient attitude.

The grace gifts of consolation, comfort, companionship, and compassion are not the exhaustive, exclusive reasons to motivate people to unnaturally humble themselves as servants. This list exemplifies the vast motives you may have in order to be broken and humble before God and people. Your list can be as long as your imagination can make it. Or, your motivation can be summarized in a single word:

Jesus.

Jesus Christ is the model for adopting the attitude of a servant. Jesus said, "Do as I have done." You should have Jesus Christ's attitude about every person, situation, problem, event, philosophy or idea, value, and possession. During his earthly ministry, Jesus Christ had the mind of a servant.

Do you?

Chapter 6

Blueprint of a Servant

‿‿‿

Missionaries three hundred years ago learned a lesson called "the principle of contextualization." Hudson Taylor was the first to implement the strategy in his work. Rather than trying to get the Chinese to dress and talk like Englishmen, he grew his hair long, wearing it in the traditional ponytail of the Chinese men. He also wore the style of their traditional apparel. He lost much of his funding from England because his people said no distinguished English gentleman could possibly dress like that. Hudson Taylor was the first to break through the darkness of China and bring its people the gospel. He understood that effective disciples reach people where they are in their language and in communication forms they understand.

Hudson Taylor's example raises interesting questions. If God is calling you to be a servant, what does a servant look like? How does a servant act? How does a servant think? How is a servant's life characterized? Scripture, teaching some of the things a servant does and how a servant thinks, declares, "Then make my joy complete by being like-minded, having the same love, being one in spirit and purpose" (Phil. 2:2).

A Good Team Player

This verse moves us from a servant's motivations to a servant's mannerisms. It lays out a blueprint, defining the servant's makeup, mindset, style, and personality. A servant is a team player. Paul strongly appealed for unity of spirit and purpose among the Philippian Christians. Paul sensed an urgency to appeal to these Christians. Philippians 4:2 hints from where his urgency originates. In that passage, two women, named Euodia and Syntyche, were having a little conflict within the church. These two women assisted Paul in his ministry in its earlier years. They were arguing and disagreeing. Their dispute threatened the unity of the entire church, so Paul appealed to them to settle their differences.

Nothing brings disdain and dishonor to the name of the Lord and his church more than internal conflict and infighting within the body of Christ. If one Christian is out of fellowship with another, that Christian is out of fellowship with God. "If a man say, I love God, and hateth his brother, he is a liar" (1 John 4:20 KJV).

> *Nothing brings disdain and dishonor to the name of the Lord and his church more than internal conflict and infighting within the body of Christ.*

Disunity and broken fellowship among the members of Christ's body are bad signs of someone's disobedience, selfishness, self-centeredness, sin, pride, or rebellion against God. Broken fellowship between two believers is a sure sign that at least one person doesn't understand what it means to be a servant. Remember, a servant gladly and willingly sacrifices his preferences, privileges, and prerogatives for the well-being of the whole body. This is why Paul pleas with us to adopt the same servant mind of Christ. When we have a true servant's spirit, we'll live in harmony with our neighbors. We'll be like-minded.

In the light of eternity—in consideration of all that God is doing—the things that divide people are usually very trivial. Paul said we need to put the trivialities of life aside and be unified in spirit. A servant doesn't push a personal agenda and doesn't fight for individual opinions. A servant doesn't disrupt or divide. A servant doesn't politic or lobby for selfish causes or ideas. A servant doesn't display anger or hostility toward people who disagree. A servant doesn't quit when others disagree or speak critically or condescendingly with those who disagree.

In fact, servants work for the benefit of the team. They speak the truth in love and share opinions gently, positively, and lovingly. They never make demands, display anger, or express hostility. Servants guard thoughts, words, and actions in order to protect the unity of the body. Those who have a servant's spirit are not so filled with pride that they think their way is the only way. They are open and tolerant of others and their ideas.

Please note, some things cannot be compromised. There are some fundamentals of faith that are not open for discussion or debate. They are fact. They are truth. The things that really don't make a whole lot of difference are the things that should be treated gently with deference.

~

No Hidden Agendas

To be a good team player, a servant has no hidden agenda: "Do nothing out of selfish ambition or vain conceit, but in humility consider others better than yourselves" (Phil. 2:3). Selfish ambition (*eritheian*) refers to a self-focused person who literally has the capacity to be bribed. When you have a servant's attitude, you do not serve and perform in order to gain something or to get somewhere. You cannot be bribed because you're not trying to get anywhere or gain anything.

Even in the church, people often work with selfish motives and hidden agendas. They "play church" for any number of reasons: to draw attention to themselves; to win others' acceptance and approval; to receive personal recognition; to move toward some position of power.

Some pastors today will start a church only after consulting extensive demographic studies in several cities with emerging populations. These pastors search for young adults with high-paying jobs living in suburban neighborhoods. They seek young families with small children and disposable incomes. They profess they are working to serve Christ, but if they are honest with themselves, they may discover a hidden agenda. They may want to start a church only if it is a potential megachurch. They may learn they're more concerned with money than ministry. They may worry more about being cutting-edge than being Bible-believing. They may be more impassioned with becoming a big name than being a nameless servant. They may have a hidden agenda, and if so, shame and pain will be the inevitable results.

~

A Humble Disposition

Not having a hidden agenda will allow you to be humble. It will keep you in the path of humble servitude. Paul said, "Do nothing out of selfish ambition or vain conceit" (Phil. 2:3). In the Greek, "vain conceit" is a compound word, *keno-doxian,* which means literally, "empty glory" (doxology).

People filled with vain conceit are easy to recognize. They seem to be absorbed in their own glory and self-promotion. They are filled with vanity, self-love, and narcissism. They carry themselves with an air of aloofness; they love to draw

> *A true servant is willing to serve in positions carrying no prestige or honor.*

attention to themselves; they love to be noticed, to be applauded, and to be recognized. True servants do not draw attention to themselves. In fact, they will try to divert attention away from themselves, pointing instead to Christ and others. A true servant is just like John the Baptist, who said of the Lord Jesus, "He must increase, but I must decrease" (John 3:30 KJV). That is the heart of the servant.

A true servant is willing to serve in positions carrying no prestige or honor. A servant is willing to serve unnoticed without applause. Servants never seek any recognition. They remain faithful because they have the heart and humble disposition of Jesus Christ.

Respect for All Others

A humble servant treats all people with great respect. This may be the most important aspect of Philippians 2:3. The word *humility* comes from the ordinary Greek word for *mind* with the adjective *low* added to it. In fact, the King James Bible translates it, "lowliness of mind." This word appears often in the New Testament, but it does not appear in any other Greek literature or writings predating the New Testament. Evidently "lowliness of mind" in the early Greek world was something only followers of Christ understood. Christians introduced "lowliness of mind" to a world of people filled with pride.

Think of Others First

A genuine servant is humble and considers others better than himself. "Others" includes people of other color, race, socioeconomic groups, creeds, or genders. We don't have to integrate the church. Jesus Christ integrated his church two thousand years ago. When a person disobeys God by refusing to fellowship with other people because they may be in some way different, that person segregates what the Lord Jesus Christ has integrated. A true servant thinks of all others with great respect. A genuine servant gladly and willingly sacrifices his own preferences and privileges for the preferences and privileges of others.

When my children get out of bed on Sunday mornings, one of the first things they'll say is "front seat shotgun buttermilk" which translates, "I'm sitting in the front passenger seat on the way to church." Then they race to the car and battle fiercely to get the preferred seat.

It would be so much more peaceful if my youngest son, Justin—hair combed so nicely, all clothes clean and tucked in, Bible carried properly, and Sunday school quarterly peeking out ever so slightly—came to the door and said to his sister: "Katie, I'm more concerned about your interests and needs than my own. I know you share my passion for sitting in the front seat by dad, and we both know I prefer sitting in the front passenger seat to sitting in the back. I gladly lay aside my preference so you can enjoy your preference." In my dreams! It's tough to visualize because that isn't the way children think.

This "others first" principle needs to be exercised all across America every day. Sociologists have already identified three generations following Baby Boomers. Those in their twenties today, the young married couples, are called Baby Busters. Teens comprise the next age group known as Generation X. These high school and college students are known as the MTV generation. The latest identifiable generation is the group known as the Echo Boomers. When we bring all the people from World War II to Generation X together into the church, we inevitably discover different generations have vastly different worldviews. Differences exist because our world changes so quickly.

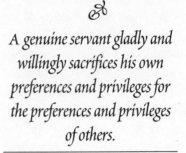

A genuine servant gladly and willingly sacrifices his own preferences and privileges for the preferences and privileges of others.

One of the areas bringing contention and division in the church is music. Some people prefer old hymns and pipe organs because that is the music they have sung since childhood. As far as they're concerned, that's the way to "do church." They grew up learning and liking this style. On the other end of the spectrum is Generation X's MTV style. They can't relate to hymns. In fact, they don't even understand the language of the hymns because the language of the standard hymns is one hundred to three hundred years old. Even if they never miss a Sunday service, they still won't know what it means to "raise my Ebenezer." Many Baby Boomers don't even know what that means. They can raise it in song one hundred times while hoping their Ebenezer is the same Ebenezer of everyone else. Nobody knows what it is because the language is so old. These words are foreign to a younger generation.

Music preference creates an issue of potential conflict. Older people say, "I prefer more hymns and organ music." Younger people say, "I prefer contemporary praise music with the electric keyboard and drums." This can frustrate a pastor. He suddenly finds himself doing the same things he would do to get his children situated in the car. He is suddenly dealing with people who issue the ultimatum, "I won't participate unless you give me what I want."

Some people attend worship services, witnessing the outpouring of the Spirit of God and seeing people giving their lives to Jesus Christ, but they can only comment, "I want more hymns," or, "I want more choruses." These poor individuals have missed the point. They should be coming to church in the same spirit of Jesus Christ. Servants should not look only to individual interests but to the interests of others first.

What a great world it would be if everyone looked to the interests of others first. If everybody did this, think about the changes that would take place:

* The next time you came to a busy intersection, someone would wait that extra moment and say, "Please, you go first."
* The next time you got on a crowded elevator and you're running late for an appointment on the fifteenth floor, someone would step back and say, "Here, you go first."
* The next time you waited at a congested checkout counter, someone would look at your load and say, "I think you have fewer items than I do, so please, go first."

What a world it would be if everyone preferred helping others above helping themselves. If we could just have the same attitude of Jesus Christ, what a world of difference it would make.

General William Booth, the Salvation Army founder, practiced the Servant Principle. In his latter years of life amidst failing health, he was scheduled to give the keynote address to the people of the Salvation Army. His infirmities kept him

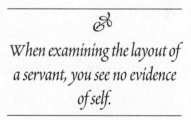

When examining the layout of a servant, you see no evidence of self.

from traveling. Unable to make the meeting, he planned to send a telegraph relaying his message to the group. The telegraph was to be read to the leaders of the Salvation Army. They waited anxiously for the telegraph from General Booth as he lay at home on his deathbed. Finally, the telegram arrived. A spokesperson opened the message and read it to the waiting audience. The message that was to set the agenda and contain the vision for the upcoming year consisted of a single word: *Others!*

The blueprints have been established. When examining the layout of a servant, you will see no evidence of self. You see somebody who wants to work with and for others. You see somebody who wants to serve and minister to others. You see a humble person who thinks of and respects others first. You see a blueprint drawn by a carpenter two thousand years ago. You see where his sweat has smudged the lines. You see where his tears have stained the paper. You see where the dirt of his hands has covered the details. Yet you see the blueprint clearly. You see it so vividly because the blood covering the blueprint belongs to the Master Architect and clearly defines the direction of service for your life.

Chapter 7

No Assembly Required

Six-year-old Curtis awoke at 5:30 on Christmas morning. Dragging his parents from their warm slumber, he jumped in glee upon seeing evidence of Santa's overnight visit. In the corner of the living room, a large, wrapped, blue box draped with an ornate red bow, beckoned young Curtis. Although it nearly drove him crazy, his parents saved that box for last.

Finally, when he thought he was going to burst from waiting, his parents let him open the gigantic box. He ran at the wrapped gift like a prize fighter charging at the opening bell. He tore into the box like a champion. The gift didn't stand a chance. Moments later, with shreds of paper strewn across the room, Curtis excitedly danced about the room when he saw the picture on the side of the cardboard box.

He shouted triumphantly, "Yes! A bike! A bike! A bike! A bike!" Curtis finished his victory lap and returned to the box. "Will you get it out for me, Dad?" he asked innocently.

Curtis's dad stood with a smile and moved to help his son. *That's why he calls me Dad,* he thought proudly. He deftly pulled open the cardboard flaps and opened the box. Looking inside, he paused.

Oops. Santa didn't do his homework. Sensing the delay, Curtis began to whine. Dad scanned the box for information. Sure enough, in small print at the bottom of the flap:

SOME ASSEMBLY REQUIRED.

Curtis may not get to ride that bike until after New Year's Day, his mother thought as she silently sipped her coffee, all too familiar with "Santa's" assembly skills.

When Jesus Christ became human, he provided a perfectly assembled model for servanthood in every action he took. He provided the model for the depth, breadth, and extent for which we should be willing to serve. When we understand the simple, succinct,

When we understand the servant attitude of Jesus, we might allow the Holy Spirit to develop the same attitude in us.

and perfect servant attitude of Jesus, we might allow the Holy Spirit to develop the same attitude in us.

Jesus = God

Jesus' servanthood is amazing to comprehend because he was equally God. The phrase "who being in very nature God," uses the Greek word *morphe*. The word means Jesus was, in his essence, God. He didn't merely have God's appearance; he was fully, truly God. Don't dismiss this point or take it lightly; Jesus was God.

As God, Jesus is eternal. He is omnipresent, omnipotent, and omniscient. He knows no limitation, restriction, or inability. There is no limit to his power, glory, abilities, justice, righteousness, strength, energy, rule, administration, wisdom, or knowledge. There is no limit to his capacity to create because "through him all things were made" (John 1:3). There is no limit to his authority. There is no limit to his possessions, for "the world is [his] and all that is in it" (Ps. 50:12). There is no limit to his rights and privileges; he is worthy "to receive power and wealth and wisdom and strength and honor and glory and praise!" (Rev. 5:12). There is no limit to his presence, his holiness, or his life. Jesus Christ is the one who designed and created everything from the atomic quark to the galaxies of the universe. By sheer fiat, through the power of his word, he spoke it all into existence. He is the very one who designed the universe and holds a billion galaxies in the expanse of a billion light years in the very palm of his hand. Jesus Christ is God!

Christ Emptied Himself

The fact that Jesus emptied himself when he became a man is even more awe-inspiring when you understand Jesus was essentially, equally God. Paul said Jesus, though equally God,

> Made himself nothing,
>> taking the very nature of a servant,
>> being made in human likeness.
> And being found in appearance as a man,
>> he humbled himself
>> and became obedient to death—
>>> even death on a cross! (Phil. 2:7–8).

Jesus Christ did not demand his own rights or selfishly grasp his own divine privileges. Jesus willingly stripped himself of his royal robes of deity and clothed himself in rags of humanity. He willingly emptied himself of the rights to his own power, glory, and dominion and took upon himself all the limitations, weaknesses, and frailties of a fallen humanity. Though he remained fully God, he also became fully human. He subjected himself to the pains, torments, temptations, restrictions, and restraints of humankind.

Though Jesus could never divest himself of his divine nature, he did empty himself of all the glory and prerogatives of heaven. Jesus, the eternal God, emptied himself of his timelessness, willingly bearing the restrictions of time. Jesus, the omnipresent God, emptied himself of his immensity, willingly bearing the restrictions of time and space. Jesus, the omnipotent God, emptied himself of the use of infinite power, willingly bearing the weakness and impotence of a helpless baby. Jesus—the perfect, holy, righteous God—emptied himself of the brilliance of his holiness, willingly bearing the full curse of all our sin, vulgarity, and depravity.

Jesus willingly laid aside:

* the power,
* the majesty,
* the glory,
* the splendor,
* the praise,
* the brilliance,
* the radiance,
* the dominion,
* the grandeur, and
* the beauty

of his supreme, sovereign Deity.

Jesus willingly subjected himself to:

* the suffering,
* the hostility,
* the pain,
* the agony,
* the filth,
* the stench,
* the wretchedness,
* the vulgarity,
* the degradation, and
* the humiliation

of fallen humanity.

In emptying himself of his dignity and dominion, Jesus became fully human. The Creator took on the limitations and restrictions of the creation. Finally, he burdened himself fully with all people's sin, carried it to the cross, and died. In his Incarnation, the infinite became finite. The eternal became immediate. The omnipotent became impotent. The sovereign became the subjected. The almighty God became a simple man. Jesus Christ emptied himself.

~

Christ Is Exalted

Because Jesus Christ emptied himself for all humanity at the cross, he is exalted. He subjected himself to the curse of a Roman cross, paying the death penalty for every person. He was buried in a borrowed grave. However, God did not leave him there. God raised his precious Son from the dead and

&

The resurrection of Jesus Christ turned the greatest tragedy to the greatest triumph the world has ever known.

seated him at his own right hand, where he had reigned with the Father from eternity. God highly exalted him, giving him a name above all names:

> When God raised Christ from the dead, he defeated all that ever defeated a human being. The resurrection of Jesus Christ turned the greatest tragedy to the greatest triumph the world has ever known. Jesus Christ rose again from the dead and God exalted him. When God looked down from heaven and saw what man had done to his son, he said, "You have done your worst. Now I'm going to do my best." When man had done his worst to God's son and crucified him, God did his best and raised him from the dead. And God highly exalted him.[1]

Jesus Christ's exaltation has already occurred. John the Revelator told about his exalted position and name in Revelation 19:11–16:

> I saw heaven standing open and there before me was a white horse, whose rider is called Faithful and True. With justice he judges and makes war. His eyes are like blazing fire, and on his head are many crowns. He has

a name written on him that no one but he himself knows. He is dressed in a robe dipped in blood, and his name is the Word of God. The armies of heaven were following him, riding on white horses and dressed in fine linen, white and clean. Out of his mouth comes a sharp sword with which to strike down the nations. "He will rule them with an iron scepter." He treads the winepress of the fury of the wrath of God Almighty. On his robe and on his thigh he has this name written:

KING OF KINGS AND LORD OF LORDS.

Jesus is equally God, yet he emptied himself. For that he is exalted. Jesus is your model; have his attitude. To follow him means to have a servant's heart. God never called you to be a celebrity; he called you to be a servant.

Part Three:

Servants, Not Celebrities

Chapter 8

Jesus Christ's Superstars

∾∾∾

It happens almost every time you click your remote control, magically bringing the blaring television to life.

click

"Welcome to 'Lifestyles of the Wealthy and Infamous.' Today we're visiting the life of Dennis Rodman. The superstar bad boy surfs a tide of popularity most people never thought imaginable. Despite kicking cameramen, head-butting referees, or cross-dressing in wedding gowns, the multicolored menace enjoys a legion of dedicated crazies who approve of his $9 million contract, flock to his latest movie, and cheer his most recent rebellion."

click

"Welcome to 'Access Entertainment.' Tonight, we've got the exclusive clips of Michael Jackson denying new allegations of sexual misconduct with children invited to his home. Later we will meet with the tabloid gossip columnists to find out who is sleeping with whom."

click

"Tonight on sports, Michael Irvin of the Dallas Cowboys answers charges that he was found in an area hotel with exotic dancers and a room full of drug paraphernalia."

click

"Christian brothers and sisters, with your 'love offering' of $500, I will take your prayer request and place it with my own hands against my chest plate of prayer armor. I pledge the Lord will answer your prayer to remove your pain, misery, or financial chains of oppression."

click

"Tonight the president faces new claims of sexual and financial improprieties."

click

The screen goes black. This is the best the television has looked all evening.

Take a roll call of our world's current superstars: Madonna, Sylvester Stallone, Roseanne, Jean Claude Van Damme, Oprah Winfrey, Ted Turner, Tom Cruise, Charles Barkley, Shirley MacLaine, Jack Nicholson, Jim Carey, Rosie O'Donnell. The list is filled with politicians, movie stars, musicians, and athletes. They can be found at most black-tie, formal galas. They parade for the photographers each time they gather to distribute awards for film, television, and song. They pose in the spotlight during sports playoffs. Call them celebrities. Call them stars. By whatever name, the world loves them.

Stars are born because of their fans' adoration. When the fans feel a connection to a celebrity, they elevate that particular celebrity to stardom. Dennis Rodman never had the following he currently enjoys when he was an average basketball player with one hair color. When he decided to abandon everything he had considered normal, to flaunt a lifestyle of promiscuity and recklessness, people loved him. Suddenly he had a gimmick, and it has made him a fortune. Though he is an extreme example, he is hardly the exception. Madonna orchestrated an exhaustively detailed public relations campaign promoting her as the "Material Girl." She presented an image oblivious to sexual taboos and barriers, doing whatever possible to become the queen of pop music. The list is endless. The world bases stardom on fame, fortune, and to a certain degree, foulness.

Oddly enough, this formula works. Fans pack stadiums to admire the stars' talent and skill. Fans are the first to defend their celebrities' multimillion-dollar contracts and the last to accuse them of any wrongdoing at times when the stars find themselves ensnared in controversy. No matter what they do, celebrities remain stars with their elevated egos, disproportional paychecks, and outrageous social, civic, and political disgraces.

Inevitably, this kind of stars fade. Eventually, every single celebrity superstar brightly shining today will wane and fade into the darkness. The world tries to remember its stars' vibrancy by chiseling their names down a Hollywood sidewalk. The world tries to hold on to their superstars' greatness by recording their feats, enshrining them in halls of fame across the land. Long after the stars have disappeared from the night's bright sky of notoriety, their misdeeds and greed will remain the lore of the ages. No matter how disgraceful celebrities may act or indiscreetly cavort and no matter how outrageously popular they become, none of this world's celebrities will ever know what it means to be a real superstar.

Despite what the world may believe, the real stars are not the people who make headline news. Real stars don't receive the applause. They don't love to hear themselves talk or brag about their own accomplishments. Real stars never decide policy. They never make a "who's who" list. They never win an Oscar or a Grammy. They never get their own TV or radio talk show. They never make a million dollars. Real stars never win an MVP trophy or a Super Bowl ring. They never play in the Final Four, the Masters, or the Stanley Cup.

> ❧
>
> *Despite what the world may believe, the real stars are not the people who make headline news.*

Take another roll call. This time, the names you read are from a partial list found in Hebrews 11. These are God's superstars:

- Abel, who by faith offered God a more excellent sacrifice than Cain, who provided him witness of his righteousness (v. 4).

- Enoch, translated by God, who found him pleasing (v. 5).

- Noah, who faithfully moved with fear, preparing an ark for his family and becoming the heir of righteousness (v. 7).

- Abraham, who obeyed God's call to go out to the land he would inherit, though he knew not where to go (v. 8).

- Sarah, who by faith, received strength to conceive and was given a child to bear despite being past age (v. 11).

- Isaac, who by faith, blessed Jacob and Esau concerning things to come (v. 20).

- Jacob, who, when he was dying, blessed both the sons of Joseph and worshiped, leaning upon the top of his staff (v. 21).

- Joseph, who, when he died, mentioned the departing of the children of Israel and gave commandment concerning his bones (v. 22).

- Moses, who, protected in infancy and raised up in privilege through childhood, was given to suffering rather than splendor as an adult, and finally, propelled into the leadership of his people because of his steadfast faith (v. 23–29).

This world would never recognize God's list of stars. God's measure of stardom is different from the world's. He measures it by faithfulness, giving, sacrifice, selflessness, and servanthood. The world says that to be a star, you promote yourself and seek fame and fortune. God says the way to be a real superstar is to have Christ's attitude as a servant.

God's superstars are people who understand commitment, sacrifice, submission, surrender, giving, abandonment, and death of self. God says the people who shine like stars are the people who give up their own rights and privileges, who humble themselves, who give sacrificially, who become obedient. God's stars live blameless, pure lives even in the context of crooked and depraved generations and do all things without complaining. While it may be tough, it is only so because we have such a firm grasp on the world's standard for stardom, which directly opposes God's standard.

When we divorce ourselves from worldly thinking and adopt the mind of Christ, we loosen our grasp on the world's way of achieving stardom and grasp God's concept of fame. Real stars serve and give quietly and unassumingly.

&

Real stars serve and give quietly and unassumingly.

They work and sacrifice and encourage and support others in the same fashion. They love the people in their homes, their communities, and their churches. They do all their service without fanfare or pretense. They are the people nobody notices. They think of others as better than themselves. They put others first.

The Christian world is not exempt from the struggle to find real superstars. Many contemporary Christian musicians no longer consider themselves "ministers." Christian musicians are now "artists" who have their own press and booking agents. These performers won't come to a church to minister the Word and worship unless that church can pay a predetermined fee, usually in the tens of thousands of dollars. Ninety-nine percent of the churches in America never hope to have one of today's contemporary Christian "artists" in their church because the musician charges more for a 30-minute concert than many churches have in their annual budgets.

A pastor can and should be one of God's real stars, but all too often he is not. These days a pastor's success is measured by his personality, his charisma, his ability to build big churches and attract wealthy members, rather than being measured by his personal holiness, his faithfulness to God's Word, and his love and care for his flock. We live in the age of the megachurch. Today's churches are the largest churches ever existing in the history of Christianity. A church's success is measured more by its size and wealth than by its doctrinal purity and its faithfulness to ministry and to the Word. We live in the age of "superstar" preachers. With the advent of televisions and mass media, we have spawned starstruck preachers willing to do and say anything to get an audience and to boost ratings. The Scriptures have been abandoned in favor of solicitations of money and viewers.

Though the Christian world may honor musicians with Dove awards or flock to the huge cathedrals to hear the most popular preachers, these

Christian performers and leaders may not find their names on God's "A-list." The true superstars are not always the pastors of megachurches, not always the award-winning, hit-producing Christian artists, and not always the TV evangelists who smile at you on the screen and promise you a "miracle" for your money.

The real stars of the Christian faith are all around us. Go to church and begin searching. They are the people who serve without fanfare, give sacrificially, and never call attention to themselves. They minister to people who are on the bottom and can never give anything in return. They are the pastors who shepherd small churches and never get written about in a magazine or get invited to speak at conferences. They are the people who visit nursing homes and retirement centers when they instead could be sitting in a comfortable seat in a megachurch. They tend to noisy toddlers so the children's parents can worship. They greet guests in rain, snow, extreme cold, or extreme heat and help guests get into the church more easily. They are the ushers who stand every week and hand out worship guides and take up the offering, doing so out of love and service. They are the church deacons who sacrifice their time visiting the sick or going to the homes of those in need.

They're the people who work scores of hours in sound and light booths, knowing no matter what they do they can't possibly please everybody. They're the volunteers who show up three hours early on Sunday morning to make certain everything is in place to create a smooth worship service without distractions. They're the people who open the doors early and lock up late. They're the Bible study teachers who, week after week, study the Word of God. Saturday nights, when the rest of the world is watching television, Bible study leaders are locked away with Scripture and the Holy Spirit so they might feed a class on Sunday morning. In a very real sense, they "pastor" their Sunday school classes.

Most people come to church every week, sit down, and leave without thinking of all the workers who make church happen. They never think of all the effort expended to clean the church, check the heating and air conditioning, control the lighting and sound, and keep everything else up and running. This work takes workers. Those workers are the real stars. The real stars are the volunteers who come before sunrise and leave after sunset to pull weeds and plant flowers. They do the work that makes the Lord's house beautiful. The real stars are custodians who faithfully vacuum, clean windows, and empty trash.

The real stars are the secretaries working behind the scenes to keep the church organized. The stars are the volunteers serving food at church fellowships. They are the people who give their money sacrificially and systematically week after week. They are the people who sit in a hospital waiting room with families going through medical crises. They are people who live a holy, righteous life at school and work, even when they are scorned and criticized for it. They are the missionaries laying down their lives on the fields of service in places no one ever notices. They are men serving as bivocational pastors.

> &
>
> *It's people like this who are the real stars, people who pour their lives out in a small town only because they love Jesus.*

I think of my own father. He is one of those bivocational pastors. Throughout my childhood he worked as a carpenter, drove a school bus, and later worked as an auditor for the Missouri Department of Revenue. He would study and prepare his sermons after the kids were put to bed at night. On Saturdays he had no time to himself. He worked so he could finance a ministry and pastor a church that could not afford a full-time pastor. Few people know of Luckey Baptist Church. Those who do are likely its members. Men like my dad are the real heroes. It's people like this who are the real stars, people who pour their lives out in a small town only because they love Jesus. They don't need any fanfare. They just love God and have a servant's heart. They don't seek recognition; they'll likely run from it. These people have a servant's heart and live a servant's life. They are the stars. God should be praised for them!

The life of a servant extends beyond the church walls. The servant can be found in the workplace and in the community and neighborhood. The real superstars, on their nightly walks, pick up the trash others leave behind. They volunteer to rake leaves from the yards of the elderly. They make meals for neighborhood families when there's sickness or tragedy.

They reload the photocopier with paper after using it. They make coffee first thing in the morning for the whole office, though no one knows who did it. They clean up their messes and do what they can to make the custodian's job simpler. The real stars take on a servant's heart, actively searching for ways they can serve their coworkers and neighbors, providing a reflection of Christ in the process.

The servant celebrity has a home too. The real servant doesn't cease living the servant life simply because church or work is over. God's real superstars never quit living the lifestyle. They remember their spouses and think of their spouses first. The real stars abandon stereotypes. Sexism doesn't exist in their households. The man will lovingly do the jobs that are stereotypically "woman's work," and the woman will tackle the "man's work." A man may hate to dust the furniture, but because he loves his wife, he will serve her and dust the furniture. A woman may hate to deal with the auto upkeep, but because she loves her husband, she'll refill the gas tank so he won't have to.

Real superstars look at situations around them the way Jesus would and serve where service is needed. The next time you feel like you have to part the Red Sea to be a superstar, think again. Just be willing to dust the living room or pump some unleaded gas into the tank.

Chapter 9

Celebrity Status . . . At What Cost?

~~~

Adam and Eve were enjoying another bright, perfect day of beautiful weather in the Garden of Eden. Birds twittered. A gentle breeze blew across their bodies. Nearby, a winding stream tumbled softly. The young couple strolled through greenery, holding hands and deeply in love. A menagerie of wildlife fed in the distance, newly named and living in harmony in God's creation. Suddenly, as Eve leaned to smell a rich red rose before her, Satan slithered by.

"Ssssay, beautiful . . . how would you like to be a ssssstar?"

The world's first talent agent led the naïve woman to the forbidden tree of knowledge. Motioning toward the tree's ripened fruit, he whispered, "For God knows that when you eat of it your eyes will be opened, and you will be like God, knowing good and evil" (Gen. 3:5).

Eve plucked the smooth fruit from the tree and rolled it in her hand. *Be like God?* she thought, *Hmmm, that sounds pretty good.* So she took a bite. Adam saw the opportunity to have it all, snatched the fruit from his wife, and chomped in. In the process, God's heart broke.

Humankind's desire for celebrity status came early in history.

In the following ages people became more enamored with themselves. Except for a small number of God's righteous, everyone completely bought into the lie of self-exaltation. Finally, God could wait no longer. He sent his Son to be the perfect example of how God intended his people to live. He sent his Son to disregard status and be a servant.

Jesus showed his attitude about status in his triumphal entry into Jerusalem. The people had cut palm branches. They were throwing their coats on the ground in front of him as he passed by. They were singing his name in praise as they welcomed their King, their Messiah.

Look closely. Here he comes. What on earth? What is he riding? Oh my! Is that what I think it is? Oh my! It is! He is making the grandest entrance of his life, and he's riding a donkey.

A donkey.

Most people wouldn't associate a donkey with a ride for royalty. Kings make entrances in golden chariots, with embossing and intricacies befitting royalty, pulled by white stallions with flowing manes. No, Jesus chose a donkey. It was like showing up at an inaugural ball in a Ford Pinto. It was like riding to the prom on an old bicycle with your date balancing dangerously on the handlebars. Jesus should have ridden in a shiny, bullet-proof stretch limousine with a Jacuzzi on the back. Or maybe, less ostentatious, a new BMW. But a donkey?

Jesus wasn't hung up on status.

Faulty Perceptions of Power and Position

Business seminars today inform management that workers prefer to have a title to a pay raise. So, if a manager is able to give an employee some big, important-sounding title, the manager will likely not have to provide a pay raise along with it! A trip to a fast-food restaurant reveals this theory in practice. Look at each name tag behind the counter. Every employee is an "assistant manager." The status of position is so important to people today. This is exactly what Jesus was talking about when he joined a Pharisee at a party:

> When he noticed how the guests picked the places of honor at the table, he told them this parable: "When someone invites you to a wedding feast, do not take the place of honor, for a person more distinguished than you may have been invited. If so, the host who invited both of you will come and say to you, 'Give this man your seat.' Then, humiliated, you will have to take the least important place. But when you are invited, take the lowest place, so that when your host comes, he will say to you, 'Friend, move up to a better place.' Then you will be honored in the presence of all your fellow guests. For everyone who exalts himself will be humbled, and he who humbles himself will be exalted" (Luke 14:7–11).

Too many people want a ministry but do not want to minister. They want a position, a title, recognition. They don't want to get down into the trenches, roll up their sleeves, and get dirty. They don't want to sacrifice and serve and work or give of themselves. Plenty

Too many people want a ministry but do not want to minister.

of people are willing to be persons of influence, but where are the people who are willing to wrap a towel around their waists and wash mud and manure off dirty feet?

Bill Wallace left behind both position and power for Jesus Christ. Bill was a successful surgeon in Tennessee. He felt God's urging and turned his back on a lucrative practice to become a medical missionary in China. At the height of tensions between Communist China and the United States, Bill was captured and imprisoned by the Chinese. He was tortured and eventually died in prison. He was buried in an unmarked grave. He was willing to go from a life of opulence to a death in obscurity, simply because he was not hung up on position or power.

There is never a shortage of people who want to make the decisions and exercise some power or control. The world doesn't need any more powerful people. The world needs people who are willing to go in and do the actual "grunt work" of ministry and service. It needs people willing to give a drink of cold water in Jesus' name. It needs people who will visit the prisoners. It needs people who will reach out to the dirty outcasts of society. It needs people who will take food to the hungry and clothing to the poor. When it comes down to it, nobody has any real power, and those who try to pretend to are only fooling themselves. The only real power comes in the name of Jesus Christ, through obeying and serving him.

~

Possession Obsession

Those who buy in to the deception of position and power soon decide that possessions are more important than servanthood. Jesus warned us: "No one can serve two masters. Either he will hate the one and love the other, or he will be devoted to the one and despise the other. You cannot serve both God and Money" (Matt. 6:24). If you commit your life and energies to the accumulation of material possessions, you cannot simultaneously serve God. You cannot be a slave to two masters. A true servant is like Paul, who learned to be content in whatever state he found himself. The question is simple, Do you have anything in your possession today that you could not walk away from or give up if God asked you to? Before you hastily answer, consider the possibility that God may have been asking you to walk away from something for a long time, but you just haven't been willing to do so.

The world is hung up on appearance, image, and perception. The world demands we have the possessions revealing our importance: clothing, cars, vacation destinations, jewelry, toys, and trinkets to accessorize our lives. Gucci. Nike. Rolex. Lexus. Brand names are more important than the product. The world is obsessed with image. This obsession leads people to run and pay inflated prices for shoes, clothing, and merchandise, simply because a superstar scribbled a signature on it. People clamor to be the first to wear the same design Shaquille O'Neal wears, willing to pay $145 for basketball shoes that will never be worn in a game. Even though the shoes won't increase the person's speed, add a single inch to the fan's vertical leap, and are likely not much better on a practical level than $40 Wal-Mart shoes, the shoes with Shaq's signature continue to be the shoes of preference. People figure that if they can't be the star, they'll buy the products that give them a star's status.

Servants select off-brand merchandise and spend more prudently. They don't idolize fallen heroes of this world because their role model has loftier standards, ideals, and procedures. Servants realize that ministry is just as effective without the status symbols.

~

Losing Life's Popularity Contest

By following Jesus and turning your back on the world's perceptions, you'll be unpopular. By denying the seduction of the image of a powerful person in a high position, you'll be unpopular. By refusing to buy possessions simply because they meet the world's elite standards, you'll be unpopular.

Jesus called you to be peculiar, not popular.

You will have to make unpopular choices and decisions, and you will have to say and do unpopular things. You won't be popular in the corporate world by taking a stand for Christ. You won't be a popular person at school or work if you

> *Jesus called you to be peculiar, not popular.*

uncompromisingly act righteous and holy. You won't even be popular in your own family when you choose to obey God over them. Remember:

> If the world hates you, keep in mind that it hated me first.
> If you belonged to the world, it would love you as its own. As
> it is, you do not belong to the world, but I have chosen you out
> of the world. That is why the world hates you. Remember the
> words I spoke to you: "No servant is greater than his master."

> If they persecuted me, they will persecute you also. If they
> obeyed my teaching, they will obey yours also. They will treat
> you this way because of my name, for they do not know the
> One who sent me (John 15:18–21).

A servant is simply not hung up on the parameters defining status. A
servant is willing to step across the line and simply serve.

Chapter 10

Mine, All Mine

〜〜〜

Of all Satan's faults, the flaw that probably got him in the most trouble was his knack for being a big dreamer. He always had dreams of grandeur and glory. He aspired to be the biggest superstar the world ever knew. He wanted to be the headliner. The star of the show. The prima donna. The big kahuna. Top dog. Boss. He wanted to be God. He was filled with pride and selfish ambition. When he tried to overthrow the throne of God, it cost him everything:

> How you have fallen from heaven,
>   O morning star, son of the dawn!
> You have been cast down to the earth,
>   you who once laid low the nations!
> You said in your heart,
>   "I will ascend to heaven;
> I will raise my throne

above the stars of God;
I will sit enthroned on the mount of assembly,
   on the utmost heights of the sacred mountain.
I will ascend above the tops of the clouds;
   I will make myself like the Most High."
But you are brought down to the grave,
   to the depths of the pit (Isa. 14:12–15).

Satan was stingy and selfish, and it cost him eternally. The temptations of self-promotion and superstardom that led Satan to his own fall are the same lures he used on Adam and Eve and the same he uses this very day. The question is: How are his tactics working on you?

Are you stingy and selfish?

If you are growing in Christlikeness, you are becoming a servant. Servants can be neither stingy nor selfish. Jesus gave up much in his extraordinary and incomprehensible move from heaven. He gave up the praise of angels and the glory of heaven. He gave up the splendor of a golden throne, the rights of absolute deity, and the expressions of eternity and infinity. He gave it all up to become a servant and eventually die for his creation.

Sharing God through Prayer and Charity

When it comes to prayer, most people are pretty selfish and stingy. Most people get down on their knees when their life is in a jam. They plead to God, "Please help me! I'm sorry for my sins. I'll try to be better. Just get me out of this fix." A servant goes to God in prayer daily and prays for the needs of others before praying for individual needs. Servants pray for the lost. They pray for the sick. They pray for the needy. They pray and pray and pray because they believe in the power of prayer and they believe in the power of God.

Servants are as free with possessions as they are with prayers, claiming no rightful ownership to anything. A servant is a steward, not an owner. Servants make no rightful claims of ownership of any-

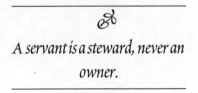

A servant is a steward, never an owner.

thing. As a servant, you know time is not your own. Your experiences are not your own because you share them in ministry. Your talents are not your own; you use them in service. Your spiritual gifts are not your own; you exercise them for Christ's kingdom. Your material possessions are not your own; you give it all away for the sake of the kingdom. Your rights are not your own; you abandoned your rights at the cross. Your very life is not your own; you lay it down for the cause of Christ.

The famous saying is "A man's home is his castle." A home is where a person eats, sleeps, and lives. A home is also where a person escapes and hides. How hospitable are you? Do you welcome people into your home to share fellowship? Are you willing to sacrifice your privacy to meet the needs of others? To a servant, a home is nothing more than a possession to be shared. Servants abandon a need for privacy and replace it with a need for service. Your home should never be a sealed castle. A servant goes out of the way to invite people over to share fellowship. There is a tremendous need today for people who are willing to sacrifice their privacy and open their homes for Bible study, fellowship, and relationship building.

Prefer to Serve

Leaving a safe home for the world of ministry requires a courageous risk. It takes a preference to serve instead of being served. Servants are willing to leave their comfort zone. Too often, Christians say they can't take part in a ministry because "it makes them uncomfortable." Jesus did not call you to a comfort zone; he called you to the cross! If you think a cross can be comfortable, you have never carried or been on one. When Christians become comfortable, the kingdom of God suffers, and the world's masses are hell-bound.

> *Jesus did not call you to a comfort zone; he called you to the cross!*

As a servant, your preferences change. The servant no longer prefers to stay home rather than go to the mission field. The servant prefers to give money rather than keep it. The servant prefers to share faith in Jesus rather than keep it secret. The servant prefers to witness, to visit the sick, to give to the poor, to help those who are mentally or emotionally ill, and to fast. You'll sacrifice preferences because you'll want to leave your comfort zone. You'll do the things that make you uncomfortable. You'll do the things that carry a personal cost. You will rebuild broken relationships. You will preach and teach. You will no longer hide comfortably in a crowd. You will wash dirty feet because you are not stingy or selfish.

You Have the Right to Remain Silent

Once preferences change, your perceptions of personal privileges will take on a new look. The average person is more concerned about his personal rights today than what is right. Doing what is right for the sake of God's kingdom is more important than your personal rights. We have the right to say whatever we want, whenever we want. We have the right to challenge those who have offended or hurt us. We have the right to defend ourselves. Even though these may be our rights, they may not be what is right and good for God's kingdom.

Paul said it would be better for the kingdom's sake to suffer by being wronged and defrauded than to bring shame to Christ and division in the body by having a brother sue a brother. "The very fact that you have lawsuits among you means you have been completely defeated already" (1 Cor. 6:7). Why not rather be wronged? Why not rather be cheated? The servant is not concerned with retribution or demanding individual rights. While a Christian may have the civil right to sue a brother in Christ, it is not a spiritual right. The right thing to do is for that Christian to suffer the loss quietly and go on trusting God to be the defense. Christians must quit trusting "self." Your own life will look totally different when your "self" gets completely out of the way.

When Jesus made himself nothing, he literally and willingly emptied himself of all his divine rights. Look to Jesus to see what a life looks like without "self." Jesus never defended himself. Jesus kept his silence, never defending himself against the false accusers before the high priest (Matt. 26:62). Jesus amazed Pilate because he remained silent, never defending himself before his false accusers (Matt. 27:14). Once at the cross, Jesus

Christ could have rightfully given a single word command, and an army of twelve legions of angels would have come to his rescue in blazing fire and vengeance. But Jesus practiced self-denial rather than self-defense.

David understood the Servant Principle. He wrote about it repeatedly:

- "My defense *is* of God, which saveth the upright in heart" (Ps. 7:10 KJV).
- "*Because of* his strength will I wait upon thee: for God *is* my defence" (Ps. 59:9 KJV).
- "Unto thee, O my strength, will I sing: for God is my defence, *and* the God of my mercy" (Ps. 59:17 KJV).
- "He only *is* my rock and my salvation; *he is* my defence; I shall not be greatly moved" (Ps. 62:2 KJV).
- "For the LORD is our defence; and the Holy One of Israel *is* our king" (Ps. 89:18 KJV).
- "But the LORD is my defence; and my God *is* the rock of my refuge" (Ps. 94:22 KJV).

How do you react to these passages? If you still defend yourself, you don't have a servant's heart and attitude. Quit usurping the privilege rightfully belonging only to God.

The Scriptures teach us that Jesus suffered and died without complaining, without griping, and without crying out against his tormentors. He suffered silently. When things don't go your way, do you find yourself giving into complaining, criticizing, or anger? A servant learns to suffer silently and even to praise God for the adversity he faces:

> Consider it pure joy, my brothers, whenever you face trials of many kinds, because you know that the testing of your faith develops perseverance. Perseverance must finish its work so that you may be mature and complete, not lacking anything (James 1:2–4).

You belong to God. He owns you. You are his complete responsibility. Whenever you complain about the inconveniences and uncomfortable circumstances in your life, you are ultimately complaining against God himself. You may think you are complaining about your boss, job, church, pastor, spouse, parents, government, taxes, or financial situation. The fact is, you are complaining against God. If you really believe you belong to the one all-knowing and all-powerful God, then you have to believe that nothing comes into your life without first passing through the grid of God's love and will for you. When you complain, you complain against God's plan for you and what he brings to your life. When life doesn't treat you like you think you should be treated, don't complain. Instead, be a servant and give God praise.

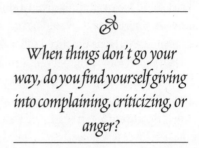

When things don't go your way, do you find yourself giving into complaining, criticizing, or anger?

Don't Retaliate . . . Redeem!

Why did Jesus make himself nothing? Why did he take the very nature of a slave? Why did he humble himself? Why did he become obedient unto death . . . even death on a cross? Jesus did it to redeem us from our sin and trespasses against him. Jesus took on our sin and suffering and bore it on his own body on the cross. Jesus said, "The Son of Man did not come to be served, but to serve, and to give his life as a ransom for many" (Matt. 20:28).

Ever since Adam and Eve rebelled in the garden, we've been repeating the rebellion in our own lives. A true statement of God's love is in the fact he never threw his hands up and said, "I've had enough!" He could have. Right-

Ever since man rebelled in the garden, we've been repeating the rebellion in our own lives.

fully, he should have. But he didn't, because he prefers redemption over retaliation.

With a servant's heart, you will prefer redemption over revenge and retaliation. You will gladly humble yourself and rebuild broken relationships. You will rather take a loss, become defrauded, and suffer ruin than take a Christian brother to court and damage the name and witness of Jesus. Christians must stop suing Christians over issues of little importance because it turns Christians into cannibals. We hurt only ourselves. We dishonor Christ because it's not his attitude and it's not his way.

Jesus did all he did in order that he might forgive us. He took the shame and the guilt of our sin upon himself and bore the consequences of our sin in his own body. He took our debt upon himself and paid it in full, so the debt could be rightfully and fully forgiven. That is exactly what we have to do when we forgive other people who offend us and become indebted to us. We have to bear the responsibility of their debt ourselves, then cancel that debt. That is forgiveness. Cancel other persons' debts so nothing stands between you and them.

Jesus taught us to pray, "Father . . . forgive us our debts, as we forgive our debtors" (Matt. 6:8,12 KJV). To refuse to forgive is to continue to harbor a grudge and to hold one liable for a debt. A servant says to everyone who causes him injury: "I'll assume the burden of your debt against me. I cancel that debt so you are no longer accountable for it. Now our fellowship can be restored."

Loosen your grasp on your privileges, possessions, and preferences of this world. You will be better able to grasp what Christ wants for your life. It's a life of sacrifice, but it's a life of reward. The greatest reward imaginable.

It's sheer heaven.

Chapter 11

My Way or the Highway

∽∽∽

Newlyweds Jason and Meredith were still learning how to live with each other. Jason hated the way Meredith made spaghetti, serving noodles in a separate dish than the sauce. His mom always served noodles mixed in the sauce. Meredith, on the other hand, couldn't stand how Jason rolled his socks into a ball before stuffing them into his bureau. She had been raised to pair the socks and to fold them neatly in orderly stacks in the drawer. Each grew more and more frustrated with the other, neither willing to change for the other.

One day they were driving to Meredith's parents' home and began arguing. She wanted to take the interstate, the fastest way to her folks' ranch. Jason insisted he knew a back route and took it instead. Now they were lost. Driving through unfamiliar country for several minutes, neither spoke to the other. Neither was willing to apologize, and neither was willing to forgive the other. As they drove past a barnyard of mules, Jason sarcastically turned to Meredith, asking, "This is your area of the woods. Aren't they your relatives?"

Meredith paused, then smiled. "Yes," she finally answered. "They are my relatives. I married into the family."

~

Servanthood Demands Selflessness

Stubborn people are impossible. They are impossible to persuade. They are impossible to coerce. They are impossible to force. They are impossible to please. Watch a stubborn child in Sunday school. Nothing makes that child happy. The child doesn't want to read a book, doesn't want to have a snack, doesn't want to watch a video. The child stubbornly wants to go back to be with mommy and daddy. The teacher tries everything, but nothing works. Not asking, telling, bribing, or begging. The teacher can only throw her hands in the air with hope that the child will come around to a friendlier way of thinking.

Too often, adults act just like that child. They want to do things their way, and nobody can tell them any other way to do it. It happens at home. It happens at Sunday school. It happens at business meetings. It happens in politics. Stubborn people are everywhere, and their attitude can be maddening!

A stubborn spirit can be a tremendous obstacle between you and Jesus Christ. Stubbornness can drive a spouse or a parent insane. Stubborn people are contrary, opinionated, argumentative, defiant, rebellious, demanding, and unapologetic. Stubbornness is combative, belligerent, and toxic to relationships. It hardens hearts and builds walls. Stubbornness is an angry proclamation of self-sufficiency and self-exaltation.

> ✃
>
> *A stubborn spirit can be a tremendous obstacle between you and Jesus Christ.*

Have a Bite of Humble Pie

To a servant, stubbornness is an alien, impractical approach to life. If you are stubborn, you cannot follow Christ's example and make yourself nothing. You can't humble yourself. Servants have no concept of self-prioritizing their thoughts, ways, or ideas above those of others. Servants are selfless. Do not misunderstand: servants do not think of themselves in a lowly, demeaning way, they simply do not think of themselves.

Jesus didn't think of himself in a demeaning, self-abasing way. He never put himself first. He knew who he was and from where he came. He did not demand his own way or force his own opinions, even though he was the omnipotent, omniscient God of all creation. Servants allow others to have opinions. Servants listen to the opinions of others, even if the others are wrong. Servants make themselves nothing. Jesus simply did not think of himself.

Low Man on the Totem Pole

Jesus willingly subjected himself to others, even though he had power and knowledge. He willingly subjected himself to others, even when they were wrong, which meant he would be defrauded, misunderstood, abused, and even killed. Servants do not give orders, demand their way, force their opinions, demand their rights, push their personal agenda, or protect their territories. They have no self-will and no selfishness left. Servants are subservient to all people in all situations. Many Christians will read this statement and think, *That's good and religious, but it simply doesn't work here in the real world. You don't get anywhere in this world by being a pushover.*

> *Servants do not think of themselves in a lowly, demeaning way. They simply do not think of themselves.*

It's true. It's not how the world operates. A person won't get any place in this world by being a servant. Just remember, you won't get any place in the kingdom of God if you are not a servant. Jesus acknowledged that his way of living was contrary to the standard of this world. In this world you toot your own horn or else it won't get tooted at all. The rule of this world is "do unto others before they get the chance to do unto you." Jesus did not live by this world's standards. He lived by the kingdom of God's standards.

God despises human pride. Proverbs (6:17) says the Lord hates a proud look. *Hate* is a strong word. Examine your life. Do you carry yourself in a way that communicates to others that you have "a proud look"? Is it in your clothing, jewelry, car, house, attitude, or personality? Ask God to take all pride out of your life because "God resisteth the proud, and giveth grace to the humble" (1 Pet. 5:5 KJV). The Greek word for *resists* has military origins. The word means "to set an army up against the enemy with full military strength." God is ready to go to war against the proud. Stubborn pride is manifested in worldly symbols if having worldly symbols becomes more important than having a vibrant, growing ministry.

~

To Love, Honor, and Obey . . .

Losing stubbornness means becoming obedient to others. Servants have an obedient spirit, being subject and obedient to the authorities God puts over us. God has established a system of authorities. Mothers and fathers are the authorities of the home. Teachers, employers, police, and government officials are the authorities of our civil structure. Pastors and elders are the authorities of our ecclesiastical systems. Obedience to authorities is a Christlike quality.

Sometimes Christians boast that they don't obey anyone. They make their own decisions. They choose their own course. They make up their own minds. They follow their own ideas. Nobody is going to tell them what to do. This attitude is a sinful spirit of rebellion. Concerning those who have authority, God says, "Everyone must submit himself to the governing authorities, for there is no authority except that which God has established. The authorities that exist have been established by God" (Rom. 13:1).

Many people in authority are not righteous. Still, God instituted a system of authorities. We may face extreme circumstances when we must choose to obey God over earthly, human authorities. Even in these situations, we must act humbly and respectfully. The person who rebels against authority rebels against what God has instituted. Those who do so bring judgment upon themselves.

The servant is easily identified. The servant isn't hung up on status. The servant is not stingy. The servant is not selfish. The servant is not stubborn.

Stand in front of a mirror. Take a good look at what makes you undeniably you. God called you to be his servant. He called you to be the world's servant. When you asked, "Me?" he gave you his answer. Commit yourself to following God. Be the servant he wants you to be.

Chapter 12

Profiles in Servanthood

∽∾∽

Not long ago, my wife Kathy was on her way home from the middle school where she teaches. She saw two elderly men across the street, both nicely dressed in jackets and ties. Because of their age and slumped shoulders, the jackets were a little large, and the collars were a bit loose. As children ran from school, the elderly men handed them New Testaments. They stood across the street because in our day, Christians can't give Bibles out in the classroom. In public middle school not all children are receptive to the gospel. They are even less receptive to two elderly men, well past retirement, devoting their afternoon to sharing the gospel. Some kids even taunted them. Still, the two men were faithful. They dressed in their best because their job was important. They knew what Jesus meant when he said we are to have the hearts of servants.

Too many senior adults think that because they've retired from work they can retire from service. These men knew that simply wasn't true. Some of the kids, by the way, did take the New Testaments. Maybe one of those boys will take out that New Testament, read John 3:16, and discover the gospel. Perhaps those men handed the gospel to the next Billy Graham! Those two men didn't know who would be accepting their New Testaments, but they weren't going to sit back in their rockers and let those kids miss a chance at meeting their Savior.

Most Christians daydream what it would be like to have been Noah, Moses, Samson, or David. But most never aspire to be a nameless, forgotten martyr, who is exiled, tortured, or executed in some remote, obscure, forgotten corner of the world. They never dream to be an old person handing out New Testaments to junior high kids who don't appreciate their effort. Have you ever dreamed for such a future? Nobody would ever make a record of you or your work or note your progress for God's kingdom. You would be forever forgotten, except in the annals of eternity with God himself. When God is needing a David or a Samson, plenty of people stand up, saying, "Sure, I'd like to fight giants, stand up and knock 'em down. I'd like to wrestle lions and be able to win. I'd like to be a famous general and turn armies around." But when God is looking for a nameless other, one willing to die with nobody there to notice, the line shortens.

The second half of God's roll call in Hebrews 11 lists some of the first "nameless others." The first half of this great chapter listed the "faith heroes." In the Christian community these people are household names. They are faith's "major leaguers." They are Abel, Enoch, Noah, Abraham, Isaac, Joseph, Moses, Rahab, David, and Samson. But now look closely:

> And what more shall I say? I do not have time to tell about Gideon, Barak, Samson, Jephthah, David, Samuel and the prophets, who through faith conquered kingdoms, administered justice, and gained what was promised; who shut the mouths of lions, quenched the fury of the flames, and escaped the edge of the sword; whose weakness was turned to strength; and who became powerful in battle and routed foreign armies. Women received back their dead, raised to life again. Others were tortured and refused to be released, so that they might gain a better resurrection. Some faced jeers and flogging, while still others were chained and put in prison. They were

stoned; they were sawed in two; they were put to death by the
sword. They went about in sheepskins and goatskins, desti-
tute, persecuted and mistreated—the world was not worthy
of them. They wandered in deserts and mountains, and in
caves and holes in the ground.

These were all commended for their faith, yet none of them
received what had been promised. God had planned something better for us so that only together with us would they be
made perfect (Heb. 11:32–40).

The "others" (v. 35) are those who are willing to go where nobody else
will, die deaths nobody wants to die, endure pains nobody wants to
endure, and do it all with a servant's heart. They are the real stars. These
are the people who now look to Christ for their example.

The treatment of servants in the Roman empire provides a better
understanding of what it means to be a servant. From the first-century
Roman point of view, a bondservant had no rights as a citizen. Also, a slave
could own no property. He owned nothing. In fact, he was owned. The
first-century slave was considered a commodity to be bought and sold. A
slave was a nonperson, simply property. A slave had no legal protection
and no court to which he could appeal when he was mistreated. He had no
jury before which he could be tried. He had no judiciary to protect his freedoms, for he had no freedoms. An owner could kill or execute a slave and
suffer no legal ramifications because the slave was only property.

To become a servant of the Lord Jesus Christ means laying aside all personal rights, placing them at the foot of the cross, and joining Jesus on the
cross. After all, God owns you. You own nothing. You are merely the steward of all God's property and assets. The world will not protect you as a
Christian. God is your only defense. Jesus Christ himself is your only advo-
cate and your only defense attorney. Paul equated the dreadful life of a servant to the descent Jesus accepted when he left heaven for his human body.
That is to be our mind-set.

Jim Elliot is just like those two elderly gentlemen who gave New Testaments to the schoolchildren. Like them, he is one of God's superstars. Jim
was a missionary. In 1956, he and four other missionaries were murdered

by the same Auca Indians in South America to whom they tried to bring the gospel.

Elliot's wife, Elisabeth, also one of God's superstars, has said: "Leaders are measured by how they sacrifice, not by how much they gain. When the will of God cuts across the will of a person, somebody has to die. Leaders are meant to be losers—losers of ourselves and losers of our rights. The best way to find out whether you really have a servant's heart is to see what your reaction is when somebody treats you like one."[2]

Let the Servant Principle consume you. What a difference it will make! Take this principle into your home and be a servant to your spouse. When husbands serve wives and wives serve husbands, marriage counselors will be out of work. Husbands and wives need to understand this simple principle. Take this principle into your church. Be a servant to the other members in your congregation, the church leaders, and the spiritually lost strangers who visit. Practicing this principle will change the church, and it will change you.

You may have known about the Servant Principle before you began reading this book. It has been around forever. Learning about the Servant Principle has always been good Bible study and preaching material, but rarely has it been put into practice. Take this principle into your home and life, live it out, and practice humility, brokenness, and selflessness as a servant. The servant is the only *real* superstar.

Part Four:

The Principal Servant

〜〜〜

Chapter 13

In the Upper Room

It was just before the Passover Feast. Jesus knew that the time had come for him to leave this world and go to the Father. Having loved his own who were in the world, he now showed them the full extent of his love.

The evening meal was being served, and the devil had already prompted Judas Iscariot, son of Simon, to betray Jesus. Jesus knew that the Father had put all things under his power, and that he had come from God and was returning to God; so he got up from the meal, took off his outer clothing, and wrapped a towel around his waist. After that, he poured water into a basin and began to wash his disciples' feet, drying them with the towel that was wrapped around him.

He came to Simon Peter, who said to him, "Lord, are you going to wash my feet?"

Jesus replied, "You do not realize now what I am doing, but

later you will understand."

"No," said Peter, "you shall never wash my feet."

Jesus answered, "Unless I wash you, you have no part with me."

"Then, Lord," Simon Peter replied, "not just my feet but my hands and my head as well!"

Jesus answered, "A person who has had a bath needs only to wash his feet; his whole body is clean. And you are clean, though not every one of you." For he knew who was going to betray him, and that was why he said not every one was clean.

When he had finished washing their feet, he put on his clothes and returned to his place. "Do you understand what I have done for you?" he asked them. "You call me 'Teacher' and 'Lord,' and rightly so, for that is what I am. Now that I, your Lord and Teacher, have washed your feet, you also should wash one another's feet. I have set you an example that you should do as I have done for you. I tell you the truth, no servant is greater than his master, nor is a messenger greater than the one who sent him. Now that you know these things, you will be blessed if you do them" (John 13:1–17).

Roads leading into and through Jerusalem were in good condition. Most rocky surfaces had been worn smooth from wind and heavy travel. Puddles were few, as rain had been light and rare. The roads were dirty and dusty. And with automobiles not yet invented, the "good" roads leading to and through Jerusalem shared one common hazard—manure.

Christ's disciples fought for road space with camels, horses, sheep, donkeys, and even goats. Try as they did, the disciples could not avoid the countless piles of animal waste dotting the trails. Animal manure dirtied every pair of bare or sandal-covered feet with thick putrid muck. Still, the disciples walked steadily toward the upper meeting room. Preparations for their Passover meal were being made. Each apostle had an agenda to present before the others. Truly this meeting would be one of history's most important "power meals."

One by one, each apostle strode through the doorway to the upper room. Each left behind clumps of brown tracks. None paid any heed to the large clay basin filled with clear water positioned at the corner of the entryway. Customarily, the host provided a Gentile servant who sat next to the basin with a clean cloth and wiped away the filthy grime from the guests' feet. However, this room had no Gentile servants.

Soon, every apostle arrived to join Jesus for the Passover meal. The initial atmosphere was somber. All sensed they stood at the verge of something significant. Yet none had any idea that each man was only hours away from having his entire world turned upside down. None had any clue to the events that had already occurred and continued to take place outside his knowledge. Judas had already conspired to betray Jesus to the authorities. Jesus would be arrested and tried in a kangaroo court later that night and crucified the next day.

In the room that night, the apostles began to make plans in the event of Jesus Christ's successful coup against the Roman occupation in Judea. All the apostles were arguing about who was going to have which position in Jesus' cabinet when he eventually established his own government. They jockeyed for positions. Concerned about establishing his own position of authority amongst the others, each apostle walked amidst his peers to argue and brag. Doing so, each left trails of flaking clods of road clay and animal waste.

Eventually, the disciples were called to gather around their Lord and Savior at the dinner table for a final meal. The dinner table at which they ate was not like the tables used today, or even like the table represented in DaVinci's classic portrait of the event. Their table stood upon no legs; it was simply a large block of wood set upon the floor. To eat, each disciple reclined on the floor, leaned on one elbow, and used his free hand to feed himself.

Jammed in a small, dusty room heated by the warm night air, the disciples ate the Passover meal. As each disciple tried to fill his stomach while dreaming ambitious thoughts of authority and power, Jesus tried to ignore the stench of the dark, muck-covered feet, only inches away from his face and food. These men weren't slobs. However, each one was so concerned with one-upping the other that he was willing to risk ruining his appetite rather than take a subjective position to the others. They would rather be disgusted by the rotten stink than be humiliated by the act of slavery. The meal progressed. The room became more heated with debates of greatness and proclamations of worthiness.

As debates escalated into disagreements and spoken words rose to shouts, it may be fair to question what motivated the disciples to leave their livelihoods and families behind in order to follow Jesus. Why did they drop everything for him? The easy answer is, because he was their Savior. Certainly, Christ's position had much to do with it.

> ஃ
>
> *Why did they drop everything for him? The easy answer is, because he was their Savior.*

The gospel accounts of Jesus selecting and calling his disciples detail that he had already begun to develop a reputation in and around Galilee before he called them to be his disciples. Crowds drew to him because of his authoritative teaching and miraculous healing. He had publicly driven out a demon from a man in the Capernaum synagogue. Jesus had healed Peter's mother-in-law. He had demonstrated his power to fishing companions Peter, Andrew, James, and John by having them drop nets in deep water after they had fished there all night without success. They then retrieved nets so full of fish that it took all four men to drag them ashore (Luke 5:1–15). Earlier John the Baptist had declared, "Behold, the Lamb of God," and many of his disciples began to follow Jesus after his baptism. All these events had evidently taken place before Jesus chose and appointed the twelve men who were his original apostles.

The easy answer is: They followed because Jesus was Jesus. Maybe— just maybe—there is a more difficult answer. Remember, these twelve men were human. Many, most, or all of these twelve, who were with Jesus on his life's final night, may have originally signed up because they saw Jesus as their way to fame. Being ordinary people, it is entirely possible that all their motives were not as pure as we might hope they would be. Undoubtedly, they all thought he was the Messiah. However, their understanding of the Messiah was far different from God's understanding of the Messiah.

Obviously, they misunderstood what God's kingdom was really about for the three years they traveled with Jesus. They thought Jesus was preparing to overthrow the Roman occupation and immediately reestablish the throne of David in Jerusalem. They thought Jesus would be king and hoped they would be members of his cabinet. Maybe these men saw Jesus as their ticket to get off the fishing boats and out of the little dead town of Capernaum. Maybe they were tired of fishing all night, cleaning fish and mending nets all day, barely making a living and stinking like fish all the time. Jesus was their opportunity to do something exciting with their lives. Perhaps this was in their thoughts, even up to the night before Jesus was to be arrested, crucified, and buried. Luke provided insight into the banter, writing, "Also a dispute arose among them as to which of them was considered to be greatest" (Luke 22:24).

Arguments began and tempers flared. Each apostle boasted of himself and demeaned his brothers. As the temperature steadily increased, the smell grew worse. Jesus had only a few minutes left to get his message through to these selfish, thick-headed disciples. He had spent three years with them, at their side day and night, teaching them the principles of the kingdom of God and trying to get them to live and act like real kingdom citizens. Unfortunately, they were slow learners. While the reek of their feet was barely tolerable amidst their loud infighting for power, position, and prominence, it was the stench of their arrogance he found unacceptable. Finally, Jesus could stand the odor no longer.

He silently pushed himself from the floor and walked to the basin. Most likely, not a single apostle broke from the intense discussions to observe his actions. When he returned, Jesus wore only a towel wrapped around his waist, and he carried the water basin in his arms. Without a word of announcement

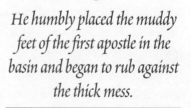

He humbly placed the muddy feet of the first apostle in the basin and began to rub against the thick mess.

or a single act of drama, the apostles' Lord dropped to his knees. He humbly placed the muddy feet of the first apostle in the basin and began to rub against the thick mess. The room fell silent as Jesus moved from apostle to apostle, subjecting himself to his servants, cleaning away both the filth on their feet and the filth of their pride and ambition. It was probably so quiet you could have heard the candlelight hitting the walls.

As he pulled each foot from the basin, the water swirled darker and darker shades of brown, while bits of debris floated in the small currents. Jesus paid no attention to the stained water. He instead focused on the clean feet of his disciples, lovingly drying each with the towel modestly covering him. When he had finally cleansed the final foot of the last apostle, Jesus looked each in the eye and solemnly stated, "I have set you an example that you should do as I have done for you" (John 13:15).

In the two thousand years since this profound moment, his message has been distorted and misunderstood. Jesus did not say, "Share this story in Bible study because it reiterates well." He didn't say, "Use this story in sermons because it captures the imagination." Jesus actually said, "Do as I have done." Christ's apostles had just witnessed the greatest object lesson in all of history.

~

Jesus Christ Is Still in Business

Jesus Christ still washes dirty feet today. He revealed that incredible truth at the upper meeting room. Hebrews 13:8 states, "Jesus Christ is the same yesterday and today and forever." The upper room gathering illustrates important insights into his unchanging nature. You have witnessed that night's unfolding events of final meals and final opportunities to teach and learn. Know now that Jesus has lessons for us to learn and understand today.

First, in washing the dirty, tired feet of other people, Jesus Christ desires to minister through you. If it is true that Jesus is the same yesterday, today, and forever, then you can know and believe that Jesus continues to minister to people this very day and this very moment. He wants to continue the ministry of washing dirty feet. His body of believing disciples are his arms and his hands. If Jesus is going to continue to wash the dirty, tired feet of people today and the days to come, he will do it through us.

How about it? Does washing raunchy feet sound like something you want to do? Disciples today are not much different from the Twelve. Washing manure off feet doesn't sound any more appealing now than it did when stepping in manure was a much more common occurrence. Just like our first-century counterparts, twentieth-century disciples are more eager to fill those "cabinet type" positions of power in the church than to volunteer for the position of "door slave." We're just like Christ's first disciples. We decide our gifts and talents don't lend themselves to foot washing. We logically reason that less noble, less able, less intelligent, or less gifted people should handle the dirty feet. We argue that we are better placed on committees, boards, or councils to contribute brilliant advice!

Serve others as he served you when your feet were so cluttered in the fetid mess of sin that they could carry you no farther.

Today is the day to change your frame of thinking. Follow the demonstration provided by your Savior, Jesus Christ. Fall to your knees and clean the sullied feet of your parents, spouse, children, boss, friends, and even strangers. Be Christ's hands and minister to the world around you. Be the source of relief and comfort for which people search. Be that voice of Jesus' good news. Serve others as he served you when your feet were so cluttered in the fetid mess of sin that they could carry you no farther.

Jesus not only ministers through you to wash the feet of others. He kneels at your feet, even at this very moment, in a loving, concerned desire to wash your dirty, tired feet and to minister to you as well. All of us mistakenly step in life's manure piles from time to time. None of us is above sin. Some moments you catch a whiff of something morally or ethically rotten. Looking down, you know the sinful mess you just dirtied your life with has you covered. You tried to avoid the sin as much as possible. Still, its filth is dirtying everything. Unlike manure, you can't go home and change shoes or wipe it away. Jesus wants to come to you immediately in those messy times. He wants to give you a fresh start and scrape the sin out of your life. When you feel tired or hurt, Jesus wants to come and refresh, soothe, and comfort you. You might be willing to die if it just meant you could have the opportunity to start over. You would do anything to have a fresh beginning.

You can—with Jesus Christ.

He gives the new beginning. He cleanses and lets you start anew. When your feet get tired and dirty, look around. Kneeling at your soiled feet, you will see the beautiful Son of God, holding a water basin, ready to bathe and soothe your aches. He will clean and comfort you.

It may be humiliating to let someone wash your feet. You have to remove your shoes and socks, showing everyone where you've been. No longer can you hide the grit, the scars, the blisters, or the odor. When somebody else bows down and washes your feet, that person can see every mile you've trod. Your feet reveal the secrets of what you have done with your life and show the person before you how many piles of manure you have trudged throughout your past. Understand that Jesus Christ is more concerned with wiping your feet clean so that you may start fresh and be refreshed than examining how many times you have ended up ankle deep in muck and mire. Drop your pride outside the door, and let Jesus Christ set you on a new path.

Many people respond to Jesus' offer as did Peter. He was too proud and defiant to let Jesus wash his feet. It is easy to be just as proud and defiant. Hearing an invitation to come to the water bin of Jesus Christ, you might think, *I don't deserve this type of treatment from the Savior of all humankind.* Just like Peter, you don't want to humble yourself. What Jesus told Peter back then still rings true today. In John 13:8, Jesus told Peter, "Unless I wash you, you have no part with me." Unless Jesus cleans you, you will have no part with him!

A terrible thing to do as a faithful believer of Jesus Christ is to exclude Jesus from the moment-to-moment needs you experience in life. Jesus wants to wipe away the small specks and smears of sin. He also wants to remove the gooey messes pulling you down neck deep in sinful misery. Don't make the

As a Christian, for you to let Jesus clean and comfort you may be even more difficult than when you admitted you needed him as your Savior.

mistake and step aside when you know your Master kneels before you in love. As a Christian, for you to let Jesus clean and comfort you may be even more difficult than admitting you need him as your Savior.

That difficulty is pride. A servant has no need for pride.

Humbly place your feet out and let your Savior minister. Let Jesus Christ cleanse you with waters of forgiveness. Let him soothe you with the drying towel so that you can go forth without stain. Allowing your Master to serve and minister to you will be the greatest, most meaningful act of humility you can ever experience.

Chapter 14

The Security Blanket

~~~~~~

At one point in time, you stood at the crossroads of your spiritual life. Only moments before, you had allowed Christ to guide your path, to clean away the grime and grit from your feet. Jesus had removed your once filthy feet from his wash basin, and he was reaching for his cloth to dry them. In that brief moment while you waited, an instant chill passed through your body.

You shivered—not from cold, but from fear. The chill was simple insecurity. For one slight instant, you feared what your commitment to Christ would bring you. You feared you wouldn't be able to answer Christ's call. You feared your best would not be good enough. You feared that you would still be weaker than the enemies, that temptations would still be too strong. More than you could have ever feared failure in yourself, you suddenly feared failure in Christ.

Before the fear could seize you in its grasp, Christ was again at your feet, completing the task he began in love. He cradled your chilled, damp feet, draping them under the warm, spotless cloth. Not only did he wipe away the cleansing water, he also warmed and massaged away your aches. The fear did not vanish; Jesus simply soothed you, chasing away insecurities. You relaxed, comforted as the punctured scars of his palms glided over your arches.

Faster than the fear could course through your nerve synapses, the security of Jesus Christ blanketed every fiber and cell of your being. You suddenly knew your best—no matter how woefully insufficient—was good enough, as long as you gave it for the glory of Jesus Christ. You knew your Savior would supply the resistance you needed from life's temptations. You instantly knew your commitment to Christ would only provide the best, most wonderful opportunities you could ever imagine. You knew beyond doubt that your only failures would come when you relied upon yourself rather than your Master.

Every once in a while, you may feel a fear again climbing up your spine and creeping over your shoulder. The moment you step out of the warm, gentle cloth of Christ's love and his will for you, fear and insecurity will reappear. Christ's security will never leave you.

You knew beyond doubt that your only failures would come when you relied upon yourself rather than your Master.

Christ's apostles must have been a very insecure bunch. They had been with Jesus for three years, but rarely had they rested in the comfort of his security. Their insecurities explain their concern with their own prestige and position. Out of insecurity, they bragged to one another and compared résumés while trying to convince one another of their own significance. They were trying to find security and significance in a life they did not have.

Jesus possessed the security they lacked. Only a secure person can strip down and perform the tasks of a servant. Only a secure person can do what Jesus did. The insecure person cannot do that which appears very insignificant, fearing such action only affirms perceptions of insignificance and inferiority. The very same security Jesus Christ had is the security Christ provides to equip you for the ministry he has planned for you. If you follow

Christ's example, you will understand how you can feel security in a culture that believes such a world is nothing more than an intangible concept.

Secure Relationship in the Father

Jesus was able to minister as a servant because he was secure in his identity. He knew who he was and what his purpose was. Jesus' identity and security came exclusively from his relationship with the Father. He did not worry about proving his significance to anyone. He never worried about maintaining his image or status. Because he was secure in his identity, he was free to minister as a humble servant.

Jesus was never concerned with performance-based acceptance. The word *knew (eido)* means Jesus knew intuitively the time had come for him to return to his Father:

> Jesus knew that the time had come for him to leave this world and go to the Father.... Jesus knew that the Father had put all things under his power, and that he had come from God and was returning to God (John 13:1, 3).

He knew of his preexistent glory with the Father, and he knew of his coming future glory with the Father. Jesus' identity was not based on what he did but rather on who he was. Who Jesus was had significance only because of his relationship with the Father. He was the Son of God, and he knew it. He could and did rest in that unique relationship. Read how Jesus previously described his relationship with his Father:

The insecure person cannot do that which appears very insignificant, fearing such an action will only affirm perceptions of insignificance and inferiority.

- "The Father loves the Son and has placed everything in his hands" (John 3:35).
- "For the Father loves the Son and shows him all he does. Yes, to your amazement he will show him even greater things than these" (John 5:20).
- "I and the Father are one" (John 10:30).
- "Don't you believe that I am in the Father, and that the Father is in me? The words I say to you are not just my own. Rather, it is the Father, living in me, who is doing his work" (John 14:10–11).

Jesus did not have to prove anything to anyone. Jesus was totally secure in his union and relationship with the Father. He was therefore totally free of performance-based acceptance. He was totally free of the desire to maintain an image before others. He was totally free of a ladder-climbing mentality.

Christ's security allowed him to obey his Father freely. Satan tempted Jesus, yet Christ's security was a barrier Satan could not penetrate. He tried to get Jesus to bypass the cross, instead wanting him to bow down and worship him. Satan promised him status and fame by giving him all the kingdoms of the world.

The people around Jesus were just as demanding and tempting as Satan. They wanted him to perform miracles for them, so that by his miracles he could prove himself and win their allegiance. Jesus never bowed to Satan's temptation of self-aggrandizement or to people's temptation that he prove himself with a miracle. Jesus never had to prove himself to anyone. His identity was already secure in his relationship with the Father.

You will never be able to minister and serve other people until your identity and purpose and security are wrapped up in a relationship of unconditional love with God. If they aren't, you are always going to be caught up in maintaining your image, earning people's respect, and performance-based

When you are secure in your relationship with God, what people think of you won't matter.

acceptance. With Jesus as your Savior, you are given a personal relationship with him. That relationship shows you that God's acceptance is not based on what you do but on who you are in Jesus. When you are secure in your relationship with God, what people think of you won't matter. You will know who you are.

You are a child of God.

You are a joint heir with Jesus Christ.

You are a saint.

A Secure Purpose in Life

Beyond his relationship with his Father, Jesus was secure in his life purpose. Jesus knew why he was here and what his purpose was. He knew the Father's purpose and timing for his life. The Gospel of John is filled with examples of people trying to get Jesus to perform some incredible miracle to dazzle the crowds, to prove his messiahship, and ascend to his throne. Time and time again, Jesus refused to be driven by their demands. He refused to do so because he knew "his time had not yet come." Jesus said to his mother, "My time has not yet come" (John 2:4). The Jews tried to capture Jesus and kill him but could not because "his time had not yet come" (John 7:30). Later, the Jews could not lay a hand on him because "his time had not yet come" (John 7:30). Finally, Jesus knew his time had come to be glorified through his obedience to the Father in death, burial, and resurrection (John 13:1).

Jesus proved a simple point in each of these situations. He was free to minister because he was secure in his purpose and he lived on a heavenly timetable. Jesus was never driven by fickle demands of people or by the tyranny of the urgent. He knew his purpose and his time. You can never really be free to serve and minister to other people in humility until you know your purpose and realize you are living on God's schedule rather than your own. Until this happens, you are going to be controlled by other people's demands and expectations. You are going to be ruled by deadlines and expiration dates. You will be shackled by "time's running out" and "do it now" mentalities. You will never be free to serve God on God's schedule as long as you are unwilling to turn your time card over to him.

How much of your life and schedule are being driven today by things you do to perform for other people's approval and acceptance? Knowing God has a special purpose for every moment of your life gives you great freedom. Knowing God has the very best plan for literally every second of your day frees you from the bondage of sinful, destructive activity. As his servant, you will be given the great desire to fulfill his purpose for your life and live on his timetable, whether anyone else approves or not. The Book of Ecclesiastes reminds us that there is a time for every purpose and a purpose for every moment under the sun. This means that God has given you enough time in your life for everything he wants you to do.

So find out what he wants and do it. Don't worry about the rest. God won't bestow upon you anything you can't accomplish in him.

~

A Secure Future

Jesus was secure in his future. He knew the cross stood between him and the Father in glory. He knew the cross was a necessary part of God's plan for him. Jesus knew that following the shame and suffering of the cross and the cold, dank, dark grave, the glory of the resurrection, ascension, and his eternal exaltation would come. Jesus knew that beyond our ugly, smelly, rotten, filthy sin he willingly took upon his shoulders waited the beautiful, glorious, perfect, loving forgiveness of the Father for fallen man. He approached the hour with confident courage. Jesus knew he would die and be buried. He also knew God would raise him from the dead and glorify him.

Jesus knew.

Shortly after washing the disciples' feet, Jesus showed how he anticipated his return to his Father in a high-priestly prayer:

> I have brought you glory on earth by completing the work you gave me to do. And now, Father, glorify me in your presence with the glory I had with you before the world began. . . . All I have is yours, and all you have is mine. And glory has come to me through them. I will remain in the world no longer, but they are still in the world, and I am coming to you. Holy Fa-

ther, protect them by the power of your name—the name you gave me—so that they may be one as we are one. . . . I am coming to you now, but I say these things while I am still in the world, so that they may have the full measure of my joy within them (John 17:4–5, 10–11, 13).

Do you lie awake at night worrying about the next business deal? Are you stressing over potential downsizing or impending contract negotiations? These may be important questions to you, but they aren't the most important ques-

Can you trust God with your future?

tions you should be asking yourself. The really important question is a simple one: Can you trust God with your future?

If you can't trust God with your future, you will never be able to minister as a servant. You will be constantly trying to manipulate your own future. You'll be working to make things happen. You'll want to promote your own cause. You'll be looking to advance yourself. You'll be trying to pull strings and network. You will simply have no place for being a servant when you are trying to get ahead in life, trying to make your own future. You won't have time for servanthood because you are not trusting God with your future.

Do you know what God has planned for your future? Are you secure in letting your future rest in him? If you are trying to manage your own future rather than trusting God with your future, you won't be looking for ministry opportunities; you'll be looking for manipula-

Only when you are able to trust God with your future will you be free to serve as a lowly slave.

tion opportunities. You won't be searching for service opportunities; you'll be searching for self-promotion opportunities. You won't seek opportunities to give; you'll seek opportunities to get. You won't desire opportunities to humble yourself; you'll desire opportunities to exalt yourself. You will have no inclination to serve people; your only inclination will be to use other people for your own benefit.

Only when you are able to trust God with your future will you be free to serve as a lowly slave. Only when you release control of your future to him and quit trying to manipulate circumstances to advance your own cause can you humble yourself to do "foot washing" ministry. Don't scheme and manipulate your own future. Don't be an opportunist. Trust God with your future. Pray and fast and seek God first. Remember:

> No one from the east or the west
>   or from the desert can exalt a man.
> But it is God who judges:
>   he brings one down, he exalts another (Ps. 75:6–7).

When you trust God with your future, you can quit manipulating and begin ministering. The good Samaritan mentioned in Luke 10 was concerned only with ministering. He, a layman, came alongside a man traveling from Jerusalem to Jericho, who had been beaten by robbers and left to die. Earlier on separate occasions, a priest and a Levite saw the man, but neither took time to get involved, each passing on the other side of the road. Only the Samaritan had compassion on the man. He administered first aid, took him to the hospital, and even offered to pay his medical bills. The priest and the Levite were too focused on their own agendas to take the time to minister to a wounded stranger. You will be just like the priest and Levite if you are driven to make your own future happen rather than trusting God with it.

Secure Individual Identity

Jesus knew his origin, and he knew his authority. He was secure in who he was. He knew he was the Christ. He knew he was the Lord of creation. He knew he had all the authority of heaven and earth. He knew where he had come from and where he was going. He was totally secure in his identity. Since Jesus was secure in his authority and his power, he was free to minister in humility. He was not worried about proving or earning his power or authority.

You may be thinking, "Wait. I'm not God. I'm not Christ. I can worry about my future. It's my right." Do you feel a chill? If you do, you are concentrating on what you aren't rather than what you are. You aren't God. But you are a child of God. You have authority: "But as many as received him, to them gave he power to become the sons of God, *even* to them that believe on his name" (John 1:12 KJV).

You are in Christ, and your identity is totally wrapped up in him. His power has become your power. His authority has become your authority. His glory has become your glory. His righteousness has become your righteousness. His wisdom has become your wisdom. His acceptance before the Father has become your acceptance before the Father. His possessions are now your possessions.

Stop believing what this world says about you and start believing what God says about you. You don't have to earn or prove your authority. All you have to do is accept and appropriate your authority; then you will be free to minister as a slave.

Get into God's Word; discover who you are. Accept it, then appropriate it into your life. The Bible says you are:

- The salt of the earth (Matt. 5:13)
- The light of the world (Matt. 5:14)
- A child of God (John 1:12)
- A branch of the true vine (John 15:5)
- A friend of Jesus (John 15:15)
- Chosen and appointed by Christ (John 15:16)
- A slave to righteousness (Rom. 6:18)
- Enslaved to God (Rom. 6:22)
- A joint heir with Christ (Rom. 8:17)
- God's holy temple (1 Cor. 3:16)
- United with Christ (1 Cor. 6:17)
- A member of Christ's body (1 Cor. 12:27)
- Reconciled to God, a minister of reconciliation (2 Cor. 5:18)
- A saint (Eph. 1:1)
- God's workmanship (Eph. 2:10)

- A fellow citizen of heaven (Eph. 2:19)
- Righteous and holy (Eph. 4:24)
- Hidden with Christ in God (Col. 3:3)
- Chosen, holy, and dearly beloved (Col. 3:12)
- A son of the light (1 Thess. 5:5)
- A holy partaker of a heavenly calling (Heb. 3:1)
- A living stone of God's spiritual house (1 Pet. 2:5)
- A member of a chosen race, a royal priesthood (1 Pet. 2:9)
- An enemy of the devil (1 Pet. 5:8)
- Born of God (1 John 5:1)

Go to God's Word and see it for yourself. These passages are just a sampling of what God says about you. Go see who you are because of God's incredible grace toward you. Now that you know how much God loves you, begin to live out of the security of your new identity in the Lord Jesus Christ. When you have that security of being in tune with God's plan, you will be able to start washing filthy, dirty feet.

Chapter 15

Just Do It

∽∽∽

Not many people know Lilly and Don Huskey. Don was a deacon while I pastored the First Baptist Church in De Soto, Missouri. Lilly and Don were truly "salt of the earth" type people. They were good, honest, kind, and hard-working. Don contracted lung cancer and went through several years of surgeries, chemotherapy, and much suffering. One October day, I looked out my church office window to one of the parking lots. Leaves had been falling from the huge oaks, elms, and maple trees surrounding the newly paved lot. Don, who had just been released from the hospital the day before from a major surgery removing a portion of his lung, stood amidst the leafy coverage with Lilly armed with rakes and trash bags. Rather than taking a well-deserved rest, they were raking and bagging leaves from the parking lot. They weren't asked to do it. No one would have known they had done it if I had not inadvertently seen them. We had a full-time custodian for such things, but Don and

Lilly were genuine servants. When they saw something at church that needed to be done, they just did it.

Don wasn't a servant only at church. He was a lifetime employee of Pittsburgh Plate Glass. If he was walking across the plant grounds and saw a piece of trash or a tool out of place, he'd pick it up and put it where it belonged, whether it was his job or not.

A servant sees a need and meets it without being asked. A servant takes the initiative. Look around. When you see something that needs to be done, don't wait for someone else to do it. Here the Christian and secular worlds can agree. Listen, in this case, to Nike. Take the initiative and just do it. In your home. At school. In your community. At work. At church.

Just do it.

The example of Jesus washing his disciples' feet is a classic. The enjoyable story is inspiring. The problem is that the fun ends in verse 15 of the thirteenth chapter of John. Clearly, Jesus is calling his followers into the job of "spiritual podiatry." Much of today's popular thought has interpreted Christ's statement in more popular, albeit less accurate, statements:

"I gave you an example that you should study on Sundays."

"I gave you an example that you should form discussion groups and meditate on them."

"I gave you an example that you should memorize my words and repeat them often."

While these are the concepts most commonly put into practice from verse 15, the only way to read it correctly is, "I gave you an example that you should do as I did to you."

Jesus is looking for action, not talk.

~

Passion for Servanthood

Christ-honoring ministry is driven by a passion to serve. A servant's most outstanding, identifiable feature or characteristic is simple service.

Many people talk about serving, yet they never actually do anything or initiate any ministry. Not Jesus. He was a servant who actually did what he said he would do and put serving others first. Jesus Christ always went into action. During the Passover meal, Jesus didn't wait for someone to say, "Hey, someone needs to wash the nasty, smelly feet in this room." After quietly surveying the situation, he analyzed what needed to be done, and he rose from the table and did it. Servants are initiators. They don't have to wait to be told what to do or wait for someone else to do it. When servants recognize a need, they simply step forward and meet the need.

Every Ministry Is Important

Few tasks were considered more humbling or more menial than the task of washing feet. Yet Jesus volunteered to wash the feet of all his disciples. Of all the men in the room, Jesus was the last one who should have performed such a demeaning task. Any one of the other twelve men should have been at the basin washing feet before Jesus took up the chore. Jesus picked up the basin and served his followers so they could learn the importance of simple service. In essence, he was telling them, "If washing feet is not too menial a task for me, even though I am your Lord and teacher, then it is not too menial a task for any of you. You should be willing to wash each other's feet as well."

You can always tell whether a person truly has a servant's heart by what that person is willing or unwilling to do. God taught me this lesson when I moved to Texas to attend seminary. Leaving behind a staff position with great opportunities at one of the largest and most exciting churches in my home state, I took a part-time position as

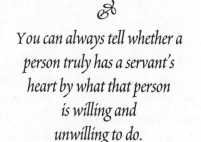

You can always tell whether a person truly has a servant's heart by what that person is willing and unwilling to do.

a youth pastor. To supplement my part-time salary, the church also allowed me regularly to mow the lawn to make extra money. The church was equipped with a small push mower for the huge lawn.

Despair covered me faster than the thick Texas humidity when I first started mowing. I thought back to the position I had left in order to come to seminary. I thought: *What am I doing here? I am a* minister, *not a lawn mower. Don't these people know how well I can preach and how effective a minister I can be?* I had a college degree. I had graduated with honors. They could get a minimum-wage person to cut their stupid grass. I truly thought they were wasting my talents and abilities. One day, while I was mowing that wet, soggy grass in 110 degree weather, amidst humiliation and discouragement, God told me exactly what he was up to in my life, using Luke 16:10: "Whoever can be trusted with very little can also be trusted with much, and whoever is dishonest with very little will also be dishonest with much."

God was saying: "Hey, you aren't the big hotshot you think you are. Right now I am testing your true mettle and character. I want to see if you really want to minister, or if you simply want to have a ministry. I want to test your faithfulness and character in something small and menial. If you can mow this grass and trim these shrubs with integrity and faithfulness, then you will have proven you can be trusted with greater responsibilities." God was also saying, "The lawn is a testing ground. If I can't trust you with a church's lawn, then how can I trust you with a church's people, pulpit, or programs?"

Suddenly, my entire perspective on cutting the lawn changed. From that day forward, I made certain the church had the best looking lawn of any building in town. No task or ministry will be too menial for a servant's involvement. A servant is not concerned about status, image, or dignity.

Certainly, it was not very dignifying for Jesus to remove his outer clothes, wrap a towel around his waist, and kneel before the disciples one by one and wash their feet. No scribes or Pharisees of Christ's day would be caught doing something so "undignified." They had to protect the image and dignity of their position. If you are serious about serving Christ and having a ministry, God will test you first in menial tasks. He will ask you to do something you feel is below your abilities and gifts, something humbling and insignificant. If you will be faithful in that which is little, then you can also be trusted in that which is much. You should also remember that you will never get too important or too big to wash dirty feet. Every once in a while, God will give you a foot-washing assignment to test your heart and your humility.

~

Preferred Anonymity

Jesus didn't make a big deal about what he was getting ready to do when he washed his disciples' feet. He gave no fanfare or announcement, saying: "Men, may I have your attention please? I am about to demonstrate to you what real humility is all about. Watch my humility as I humbly perform this menial task to each of you who think you are so important."

Some people today can be so proud about how humble they can be. These are the type of people who wish they could write a book entitled *My Humility and How I Got It!* Jesus never worked this way. He simply stood unannounced, quietly slipping out of his tunic. He wordlessly moved from man to man. He untied each man's sandals, placing his feet in the basin of water, and gently massaging the dirt, manure, and grime off of every foot. He finished by softly drying each man's feet with the towel around his waist. He ended as quietly as he had begun. In the process, his actions spoke more loudly than words.

A servant doesn't need a glowing introduction. A servant doesn't need a trumpet to blow just before beginning a ministry. A servant just reaches out and ministers. No fanfare. No recognition. Ministry is always more important than the minister. Service is always more important than the servant. A servant doesn't need applause for the ministry or service. A true servant has developed the ability to minister and serve with joy, whether anyone notices or not.

> *A true servant has developed the ability to minister and serve with joy, whether anyone notices or not.*

～
Strength Without Limitations

A servant knows his gifts and strengths but refuses to be limited by them. Jesus, the eternal, almighty God, always knew he was the Lord over all creation. Jesus did not serve as the "foot-washing slave" because his job description mandated it. He did it despite his office. Jesus knew his strengths, yet he refused to be limited by them. He did not cling to his power and glory. Instead, he humbled himself. Jesus could have rightfully refused the incarnation. He could have said "no thanks" to the humiliation and passed on washing dirty feet. He could have vetoed the whole concept of the cross. He could have taken a rain check on the torture. He could have nixed the idea of the indignity. All this was below his dignity and his authority. Yet, in his heart, Jesus was a servant. He was willing to step down from his office and his rights and privileges. He was willing to humble himself and literally "make himself nothing." He knew who he was but refused to let himself be limited by it.

In our day of specialization, the enemy subtly tricks us to use our gifts, talents, and strengths against us. We become so specialized that we lose sight of what God has called us to do. God never called us to be specialists. He called us to be servants. If we are not careful, Satan will use some very helpful tools we have in the church today against us. Spiritual gift inventories and personality inventories can be as dangerous as they can be helpful in discerning ministry opportunities. While there is some benefit in knowing your spiritual gifts and understanding your personality traits, there is also the risk that those tools may be used to hide the dire sin in your life. Don't let your specialties or gifts limit you in your obedience to ministry. Don't use those tools as excuses for disobedience or unwillingness to minister in basic acts of service. Those tools should only be used to reveal how much we all need Christ to change us and make us bigger than our specialties.

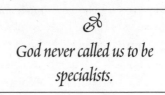

God never called us to be specialists.

Don't become so enamored with your unique spiritual gifts that you lose sight of the fact that we are all called to be servants. The statements are common and overused: "I can't work in the nursery; my spiritual gift is teaching," or, "I can't serve as a greeter; I'm too shy." It doesn't matter what your gift or personality is, you are called to love all people. You are called to care for all people. You are called to reach out to all people. You are called to serve all people. You are called to minister to all people. You are called to wash dirty feet.

If the gathering in the upper room were to take place today, Christ would still have taught, "You are to do as I have done and wash each other's feet." Peter, though, may have had a more contemporary response:

"Well, Lord, I'm afraid I can't do that. You see, I recently took a really neat test called a personality inventory. I discovered I have a 'Type A, Choleric, ITFJ personality.' I am outspoken, hot, impetuous, and driven. I am leadership material. So foot washing does not really fit my personality. Also, I just took this cool spiritual gifts inventory. I discovered I have the gifts of prophecy and exhortation. Maybe you ought to contact John about this foot-washing work. You see, he is a much more sanguine personality, and he has the gift of service ministry. Sorry, Jesus, but surely you can see this foot-washing opportunity just doesn't fit me."

Knowing your specialty is important, but don't ever be limited by that knowledge. Don't let that knowledge keep you from actively serving daily.

Chapter 16

Driven by Love

෨෨෨

W hen Kathy and I accepted the dinner invitation extended by a married couple who were relatively new members of the church, we had no idea that later that evening we would get to see one of the world's great pyramids. The pair invited us because, they said, they wanted to show their appreciation and express their thanks for how God had used the church in their lives. We love these types of opportunities to meet with people in a more personal setting. We were so much looking forward to a cordial night of fellowship and new friendship.

The meal was fabulous. The conversation was delightful. After the final course was served and the dishes were being carried to the kitchen, the entire nature of our visit changed.

Their true motive for inviting us to dinner was to enlist us in the pyramid marketing business in which they were involved. They wanted me to use my position as pastor to influence the members of Riverside to join as well. We declined as politely as possible and went home

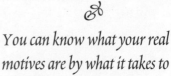

You can know what your real motives are by what it takes to stop you from serving.

terribly disappointed. The ache in our stomachs was far more nauseating than any case of food poisoning.

We soon found out that the couple had been "mining" their Sunday school class for prospects to join their business. They were using their church to make professional contacts and to increase their revenues. Their actions saddened me and caused me to question every motive they may have had and every activity in which they participated.

What motivates you? What drives you to minister and serve? What motivates you to sing in the choir, teach your class, serve as an usher, work on a church staff, or even to attend church? Check your motives. Are you serving purely because you are driven by the consuming love of Jesus Christ, or do you have some selfish motive in your heart? Are you serving with the hope of getting a sense of personal accomplishment? Are you hoping to be applauded and recognized? Is your desire to be noticed and appreciated? Are you trying to establish your identity? Are you looking for personal satisfaction? Are you wanting to feel loved and accepted? You must always check your motives, even daily. You must make sure you are doing what you do simply because you have been captured by Christ's love and you love him.

You can know what your real motives are by what it takes to stop you from serving. If you quit because someone offends you or hurts your feelings, because you are never noticed, because someone angers you, because you don't get your way, or for any reason other than God's leading, your real motive was not love. It was a selfish motive. Too many people have left or quit a church or the ministry because someone hurt their feelings. When you check your motives, you may be surprised by what you discover.

Selfless love drives all Christ-honoring ministry and is the only acceptable motive for service. Paul was absolutely bound by Christ's love. He could not escape Christ's love; it drove him to lay down his life in reckless abandon to the Lord. "For Christ's love compels us, because we are convinced that one died for all, and therefore all died" (2 Cor. 5:14).

Active Love

Jesus Christ's love was active love. When he took the basin and towel and washed his disciples' feet, Jesus actively demonstrated his love. Jesus had talked and thought a lot about love. Now he showed it. Genuine love is always active. It is demonstrated in deeds of kindness, in acts of thoughtfulness, in moments of sacrifice, and in times of generosity. Love is not something you talk about; it is something you do. Love is a verb.

Inexhaustible Love

Jesus Christ's love was inexhaustible. The King James Version translates John 13:1 as, "He loved them unto the end." The point is not that he loved them to the end of his life but that he loved them to the uttermost degree possible for him to love them. Jesus loved those men as much as it was possible for them to be loved. His love was inexhaustible. No one could have loved them more than he loved them. No measure of love could have been greater. If you belong to Christ right now, no one in the world loves you more than he. Remember his love amidst the changing tides of your life. Remember, Christ is in control. Nothing can possibly come into your life without first being filtered through the inexhaustible love of Jesus Christ.

Unconditional Love

Jesus Christ's love was unconditional. People often forget that amidst all the feet that Jesus cleaned was a pair belonging to the betraying man who would hand him over to the authorities to be crucified. Nonetheless, he lovingly washed the feet of Judas. In all likelihood, the path Judas took leading to the upper meeting room originated at the location of the betrayal (see John 13:2). Jesus knew where the dirt on Judas' feet came from. After he served bread to his disciples, he instructed Judas, "What you are about to do, do quickly" (John13:27).

Judas was there, and Jesus washed his feet.

Jesus cleansed the filthy feet of the filthy man who plotted the filthiest betrayal.

While it had to be hard to wash the feet he knew would soon be running to his enemies to betray him, he still demonstrated his love for Judas. If it had been anybody else with the same foreknowledge, the scene would have likely been much different. If anybody else had

> ॐ
>
> *Jesus washed the feet of the one who was betraying him because his love was unconditional.*

been in Christ's place, the other eleven disciples would have all received a foot washing. When it was Judas' turn, anybody else would have dunked his head in that filthy water and held him under a while. This wasn't how Jesus operated. Jesus washed the feet of the one who was betraying him because his love was unconditional. Christ's unconditional love is the only way to explain how Judas could sprint through the night to betray his Lord with freshly cleaned feet.

Can you do what Jesus did? Can you wash the feet of those who betray, violate, or hurt you? Can you cleanse the feet of a person who deceived you, cheated you, or used you? Can you wash the feet of the "Judases" in your life? This is the ultimate test of whether you have a servant's spirit. When someone hurts you or offends you, can you take the initiative and return that act of betrayal and injustice with an act of kindness and ministry? Scripture exhorts:

> Do not repay anyone evil for evil. Be careful to do what is right in the eyes of everybody. If it is possible, as far as it depends on you, live at peace with everyone. Do not take revenge, my friends, but leave room for God's wrath, for it is written: "It is mine to avenge; I will repay," says the Lord. On the contrary:

"If your enemy is hungry, feed him;
if he is thirsty, give him something to drink.
In doing this, you will heap burning coals on his head."
    Do not be overcome by evil, but overcome evil with good
(Rom. 12:17–21).

Also:

But I tell you: Love your enemies and pray for those who persecute you (Matt. 5:44).

Take the person who cheated you on a business deal to lunch. Forgive
the person who dents your car. Invite to dinner the opponent stealing your
business. Buy a gift congratulating the one taking your job. Speak well of
those who criticize you. Bake a pie for the neighbor who allows his pet's
waste in your yard. Send a card or flowers to the boyfriend or girlfriend
breaking up with you. Even if your ex is suing you for more money, volunteer to go over and help with the house painting. Everybody has a Judas in
life. Everybody has received a raw deal at least once in life. How can you
wash the feet of your Judas? Are you even open to the suggestion? You may
think it will kill you to go to that person who betrayed you, cheated you,
abused you, who hurt you so deeply. But Jesus said, "Now that you know
these things, you will be blessed if you do them" (John 13:17).

Have courage. You will need a lot of it to obey Christ in this endeavor. If
you do, you will receive the greatest joy and satisfaction you have ever
known. Moreover, your active display of love will also be the most powerful Christian witness to the offending person that you could possibly provide. It will open your life and heart for tremendous blessing from God
himself. It will set you free from any bitterness or anger. It will lift you from
depression and flood your life with joy. If God tells you to wash the feet of
someone who betrayed or hurt you, and you sense resistance, repulsion, or
refusal at the thought, take a moment to determine from where your resistance originates. Either it comes from your enemy, Satan, or from your
flesh, and it's sinful pride.

The time has come. Go. Do what your Savior did two thousand years ago.
Wash the feet of the Judas in your life!

Part Five:

The Suffering Servant

Chapter 17

The Will to Suffer

❦❦❦

Look around you; all is falling apart. Literally. Friends don't come around as often. You have been getting a lot of pressure at work. Money is suddenly tight. All your plans have fallen apart. If something could break, it has broken. If something else *could go* awry, it has. If even one small thing *could* go your way, it hasn't. Why in the world are you suffering so much? All you did was kneel at the cross of Jesus Christ and call him Savior.

You finally made the commitment. You turned everything over to God: life, finances, relationships, worries, plans, hopes, dreads. You took the steps to start living for him: you poured out all the booze; you started going to church on a regular basis; you began reading the Bible daily. You set your first steps on the path of following Christ, yet you suddenly feel yourself tossed about in a twisting tornado of confusion, misfortune, and oppression. Almost instantly following your salvation, you experience a tremendous onset of miserably tough times. You think, "When I was going along with Satan, doing things my own way, everything seemed to run smoothly. It was when I tried to get right with God that things went haywire."

Many people mistakenly think that when they surrender their hearts and lives to Jesus all their problems will suddenly be solved. They think they will never again experience any darkness or storms in life. They believe every day will be filled with sunshine, convinced they will never again have to deal with adversity, and all will be hunky-dory. They believe in their hearts that they will suddenly become exempt from pain and suffering because Jesus now resides in them.

What a beautiful thought. The only problem is that it simply isn't true.

Ironically, the very opposite may be true. When you gave your life to Jesus Christ, you may very well have opened yourself up for problems and pains you had never known before. At salvation, you immediately inherited a brand new set of enemies. You suddenly became an enemy of this present world system. The Bible says that you, as a Christian, are a foreigner in your own world. Jesus said if the world hated him, surely it will hate you. You stand out. You are different. You live in a world that is antichrist. When you became a Christian, you discovered you would never again find it comfortable living in this world. As long as your faith in Christ defines you to the world, you will be the enemy of Satan and every demon under his dominion. Scripture addresses the battle you will face as a Christian:

> Finally, be strong in the Lord and in his mighty power. Put on the full armor of God so that you can take your stand against the devil's schemes. For our struggle is not against flesh and blood, but against the rulers, against the authorities, against the powers of this dark world and against the spiritual forces of evil in the heavenly realms. Therefore put on the full armor of God, so that when the day of evil comes, you may be able to stand your ground, and after you have done everything, to stand (Eph. 6:10–13).

The day of evil is not some distant day yet to be endured. That evil day will inevitably come because you have chosen to follow Christ. That day may come again and again, repeatedly challenging you with temptations and tough choices. Every day you need to be equipped with the armor of God. If the day of evil has not yet come, it is undoubtedly barreling toward you on your life's calendar, hoping you are not prepared, and ready to strike you down like a bowled-over set of tenpins.

You need to prepare, so that when your day of evil does come, you can stand. Don't be surprised when the closer you get to God the hotter the battle becomes. In football, the battle gets more fierce the closer the offense gets to the goal line. Once at the five-yard line, the offense fights and scrapes for inches, not yards. The battle of your life becomes more intense as you move toward the goal line in your Christian walk. The more you grow to be like Christ, the more fierce will be the onslaught from the enemy. Jesus Christ said, "Whoever serves me must follow me; and where I am, my servant also will be. My Father will honor the one who serves me" (John 12:26). If you are going to become his servant, you must be willing to go where he goes.

Don't be surprised when the closer you get to God the hotter the battle will become.

Jesus was a suffering servant. If you are serious about following Jesus, you also will become a suffering servant. Jesus made no secret of the fact that by following him you will open yourself up for suffering and persecution. Jesus did not promise financial security and prosperity to his followers. The Scriptures, however, do promise suffering and persecution:

> Dear friends, do not be surprised at the painful trial you are suffering, as though something strange were happening to you. But rejoice that you participate in the sufferings of Christ, so that you may be overjoyed when his glory is revealed. If you are insulted because of the name of Christ, you are blessed, for the Spirit of glory and of God rests on you. If you suffer, it should not be as a murderer or thief or any other kind of criminal, or even as a meddler. However, if you suffer as a Christian, do not be ashamed, but praise God that you bear that name (1 Pet. 4:12–16).

Be aware of the adversity coming in your life, so you will not be surprised when it flows over you like a tidal wave. Expect it, so you will not be discouraged and will stand tall, living your life for the Lord. Deal with it, so you will understand how God uses suffering and adversity in your life. Respond to it when you are caught up in the midst of great pain and hardship. We live in an age of rampant, covert persecution, but we may be standing on the brink of a period of very overt persecution. The first waves of blatant persecution wash toward us daily. These small cresting splashes of oppression may only uncomfortably soak our socks right now, but they are the first waves of the impending tidal wave. It is coming, and it will not cease until we are submerged and fighting for our lives.

Moses was one of God's great servants, and he suffered. "Now Moses was a very humble man, more humble than anyone else on the face of the earth" (Num. 12:3). Even though Moses was a meek, humble, faithful servant of the Lord, he faced great hardship and suffering in his life:

> *Despite the fact that Moses had a true servant's heart, the Scriptures reveal that he understood what it meant to suffer pain and hardship in his life.*

> By faith Moses, when he had grown up, refused to be known as the son of Pharaoh's daughter. He chose to be mistreated along with the people of God rather than to enjoy the pleasures of sin for a short time. He regarded disgrace for the sake of Christ as of greater value than the treasures of Egypt, because he was looking ahead to his reward (Heb. 11:24–26).

Despite the fact that Moses had a servant's heart, the Scriptures reveal that he understood what it meant to suffer pain and hardship in life. His example demonstrates that the decision to be a suffering servant of Jesus Christ is one that requires willful, deliberate consideration.

Men and women of faith make a cognizant, rational decision to be servants of Christ and to suffer with him, even unto death. The Bible says

Moses made a choice "to be mistreated along with the people of God rather than to enjoy the pleasures of sin for a [season]" (Heb. 11:25).

Moses' story is one of the first taught in Sunday school. His parents were Hebrew slaves in Egypt, all of whom were treated terribly at the time. Following Pharaoh's decree curbing their population growth, all Hebrew male infants were immediately put to death the moment they left the womb. Moses' parents knew God had a plan for their little boy, so they refused to kill him. Instead, they hid him in a basket along the Nile river. Pharaoh's daughter came to the Nile to bathe, found the basket, and fell in love with the baby Moses. Pharaoh's daughter adopted Moses as her own son and raised him in all the wealth and opulence of the court of the king who ruled the world. Moses' own biological mother, Jochebed, was hired to care for Moses in his younger years. She taught him about their heritage, and more importantly, about Jehovah God. She planted in him a moral foundation that was with him for the rest of his life. Moses was educated in the best schools. He grew up as the Pharaoh's grandson. He was a prince. He was royalty, destined someday to inherit the throne and rule the known world.

Before that day came, another day arrived, a day on which Moses had to make a choice: continue enjoying all the wealth, privileges, and power of an Egyptian pharaoh, or walk away from it all and follow the God of his forefathers, identifying with his people, the Hebrew slaves. After he thought about it, he chose to follow God. He chose to become a slave. He chose to walk away from all the opportunities of the kingdom of Egypt. He chose obedience to God.

Moses made this decision when he was forty years old. This was not a radical, youthful, idealistic decision. This was the decision of a mature, seasoned man. You may be just like Moses. You may have spent your adult life just like Moses. You have enjoyed life in the fast lane, living in the corporate world, making it big in business. You climbed the ladder and accumulated material wealth at each stop. Do not forget the question Jesus asked, "What shall it profit a man, if he shall gain the whole world, and lose his own soul?" (Mark 8:36 KJV). This was not a rhetorical question. Christ demands an answer to that question from each and every person. If you are in your mid-life years, it is not too late to make the choice Moses made. It is not too late to choose Christ rather than choosing the world.

~

Looking with an Eternal Perspective

Moses chose to suffer as a slave rather than reign as a king because he understood the concept of deferred gratification. He chose to be mistreated and to suffer with the people of God. In the end, he enjoyed eternal glory. He passed on enjoying the pleasures of a season

> *Whenever you choose sin, it is always a shortsighted decision. Take the long look.*

of sin. Moses took the long look. The pleasures of Egyptian royalty were only temporary. The glory and pleasures of God and heaven are eternal.

The Bible does not deny that sin is fun and pleasurable for a season. However, the ultimate results of sin are deadly. Sexual promiscuity, the party life, making money at all costs, sacrificing ethics and morals—in each case, the long-term consequences are deadly.

Whenever you choose sin, it is always a shortsighted decision. If you are sexually promiscuous, you need to take the long look. If you're neglecting your marriage for the benefit of work, take the long look. If you're being tempted to cheat on your spouse, take the long look. If you are considering abortion, take the long look. If you are experimenting in drugs or alcohol, take the long look.

If you are sinning, you are not looking to the future. You are not seeing the long-term consequences. Don't sell out your long-term future for a short-term pleasure.

Take the long look.

Do you remember those in the Bible who refused to take the long look and made shortsighted decisions? In every case, the shortsighted decision was one these people paid for the rest of their lives. Adam and Eve made a shortsighted decision when they saw the fruit of the tree and took some and ate it (Gen. 3:6). Their deadly decision impacted all humankind. David made a shortsighted decision when he looked at Bathsheba with lust and decided to commit adultery with her. His deadly decision ruined his family. Samson made a shortsighted decision when he laid his head on Delilah's lap. Achan made a shortsighted decision when he stole gold from the spoils of Jericho and hid it under his tent. His decision brought death to the camp. Judas made a shortsighted decision when he sold Jesus out for thirty pieces of silver. King Agrippa made a shortsighted decision when he said to the apostle Paul, "Paul, Almost thou persuadest me to be a Christian" (Acts 26:28 KJV). Don't make the shortsighted decision. You may feel good and happy temporarily, but in the long run, it will be a deadly decision.

~

Stop, Think, Act

Moses chose to suffer as a servant because he also understood the concept of deliberate evaluation. To comprehend the full measure of Moses' sacrifice, you have to have an image of the opulence and wealth of Egypt during his day. Archeological discoveries, such as the tomb of King Tutankhamen (King Tut), who lived only one hundred years or so after Moses, have revealed how vastly rich Egypt was at its apex. No doubt Moses had access to this wealth and was likely in possession of much of it. But God's Word says Moses "regarded" disgrace for the sake of Christ as of greater value than the treasures of Egypt. The word translated *regarding (hegeomai)* speaks of a careful, thoughtful, well-evaluated decision. This was a decision weighing all the pros and cons. Moses weighed what Egypt had to offer and what God had to offer and decided God offered a much better deal. The words translated *greater value (mega plouton)* are very descriptive words, meaning the disgrace for the sake of God was of immense, immeasurable, incomparably greater value than the treasures of Egypt. It wasn't even close. God's deal was a lot better. God always offers more than what this world can offer.

From the world's standpoint, Moses sacrificed everything for nothing. From a spiritual standpoint, Moses sacrificed nothing for everything. If you make a careful, measured evaluation of your options, you will discover the same thing Moses discovered: God's deal is always the best deal. Though the initial decision to choose for God today may be at first painful and humbling, it pays the highest dividends in the long run. You choose to suffer as a servant of Christ because of deferred gratification and because of deliberate evaluation.

If Moses had chosen Egypt, he wouldn't have shocked the world. He would have done what the Egyptians would have done, exactly what they expected him to do. But would you remember him? How many Egyptian pharaohs can you name aside from the recently mentioned King Tut? If Moses chose the path of least resistance, he would have died in obscurity. He would have made no impact and no difference on this world.

Instead, Moses followed God. Go virtually anywhere in the world and meet with people from any one of the world's three great religions. The name *Moses* is known and is spoken with great reverence. Moses made the right decision.

The decision Moses made is the same decision you make every day. When you chose to forego buying a new car or remodeling your house to give discretionary money to your church's building program, you made that decision. You made the choice when you abandoned a lucrative, comfortable business career to give your life to Christ's work in the mission field. You made the choice when you decided not to cheat, lie, or deceive people to get ahead. You made the choice when you quit using foul language or laughing at dirty jokes to fit in at work. You made the choice when you stopped climbing the corporate ladder and instead invested your life in family, friends, and kingdom ministry. You make the decision every time you stand for Christ amidst a secular world. You make the costly choice when you leave your secular career to pursue the call of God to vocational ministry. You face the choice when you turn off the television to spend time in God's Word. You face the choice when you go to church rather than oversleep. You face the choice when you witness for Christ, no matter what other people think. You face the choice when you date only other Spirit-filled believers, so you and the person you marry will never be unequally yoked. You make the choice when you refuse evolution's lies and publicly stand for God, inviting scorn upon yourself.

Every time you decide to obey God rather than take the path of least resistance the world offers, you make the same choice Moses made. You face the same decision a thousand times in a thousand different ways every day in your life. If you deliberate for a bit and look with an eternal perspective, is the decision so difficult after all?

Chapter 18

A Myriad of Martyrdom

∽∽∽

The entire two thousand years of Christian history have been written in the blood of Christian martyrs. It has been a two-millennia history of persecution, tortures, executions, and bloodbaths. Today, the central symbol representing the Christian faith is a Roman cross, the most cruel, torturous tool of death the people of that generation could create. Torture, murder, death, and martyrdom have been—starting with the death of Jesus Christ himself—and continue to be common endings to faithful Christians.

Church tradition suggests that every single one of Jesus Christ's original twelve disciples died horrible deaths. Matthew was slain in Ethiopia. Mark was dragged through the streets until he was dead. Andrew was tied to a cross. James was beheaded. Philip was crucified and stoned. Bartholomew was flayed alive. Thomas was pierced with lances. James the Lesser was thrown from the temple and beaten to death. Jude was shot to death with arrows. Matthias was stoned. Peter was crucified upside down because he felt unworthy to be crucified in the same manner as Christ. Then Paul was beheaded.[3]

Shortly after Christ's closest followers were mercilessly slaughtered around the end of the first century, a public campaign of hate was successfully waged against Christians throughout the Roman Empire. Christians were blamed for every problem and crisis in the empire. They were perceived as the foremost of the state. The empire carefully orchestrated a successful effort of "social engineering." Very soon, every people group in the empire began to have one common enemy.

Christians.

On June 18, A.D. 64, Emperor Nero burned his own capital city of Rome to ashes. He blamed Christians for the devastating inferno. Soon, Christians were being dragged into the Roman amphitheaters, tortured to death, and fed to wild beasts while the public viewed from balconies, cheering their brutal slaughter.

Relentless persecution of Christians spread throughout the empire. Christians were beaten to death. Beheaded. Hanged. Burned at the stake. Fed to wild animals. Dragged to death. Boiled, flayed, or skinned alive. Disemboweled. Their properties were confiscated by state authorities. They were forced into slavery. Children were taken from parents and sold into slavery, never to be reunited.

The same successful campaign of deception and hate is being waged against Christians today in many places throughout the world. Persecution did not only take place two thousand years ago. An estimated 100 million Christians have been martyred for their faith during the twentieth century. More Christians have been martyred worldwide during this century than the nineteen centuries that preceded it. More than 150,000 Christians are martyred for their faith every year around the world. Today, in the Sudan, forces from the Islamic government frequently raid the southern villages, killing Christian men and selling Christian women and children into slavery. China holds more Christian prisoners than any other nation in the world. An American Bible Association missionary recently returned from there, testifying she had seen a public arrest warrant being circulated by the Chinese government's security bureau. The names of three thousand evangelical pastors were on that warrant.[4]

You may think it can't happen in America. Don't be deceived. What is happening to millions of Christians around the world today likely will happen here soon. The world's policy toward the treatment of Christians has not changed in two thousand years. This is no radical, paranoid position. Open your eyes and look at the world around you. It is happening right now. America is moving so quickly in this direction as a society that it is frightening.

Americans don't realize we have enjoyed an unprecedented three-hundred-year parenthesis in history with little persecution. We must not forget that relentless religious persecution drove our forefathers to this land to carve a new society out of the wilderness. The idea of "those who don't remember the lessons of history are destined to repeat it" rings true. More and more Americans are forgetting God. Those who remember him suffer persecution under those who have forgotten him. Persecution is coming sometime in your life, no matter how much you'd like to avoid it. "In fact, everyone who wants to live a godly life in Christ Jesus will be persecuted" (2 Tim. 3:12). As a servant and follower of Jesus Christ, you are considered an enemy of this current antichrist world system. The world system hates Christ, and it will hate you as well:

> *Americans don't realize we have enjoyed an unprecedented three-hundred year parenthesis in history with little persecution.*

> If the world hates you, keep in mind that it hated me first. If you belonged to the world, it would love you as its own. As it is, you do not belong to the world, but I have chosen you out of the world. That is why the world hates you. Remember the words I spoke to you: "No servant is greater than his master." If they persecuted me, they will persecute you also. If they obeyed my teaching, they will obey yours also. They will treat you this way because of my name, for they do not know the One who sent me. If I had not come and spoken to them, they would not be guilty of sin. Now, however, they have no excuse

for their sin. He who hates me hates my Father as well. If I had
not done among them what no one else did, they would not be
guilty of sin. But now they have seen these miracles, and yet
they have hated both me and my Father. But this is to fulfill
what is written in their Law: "They hated me without reason."
I have given them your word and the world has hated them,
for they are not of the world any more than I am of the world
(John 15:18–25; 17:14).

Today it is "politically correct" to promote tolerance and special pro-
tective rights for any and every group, belief, and lifestyle imaginable.
Different "politically correct" groups enjoy unprecedented protection:
groups advocating gay rights; groups wanting rights for satanic cults and
witchcraft; groups demanding rights for radical, militant Islamic groups,
such as that led by Louis Farrakhan; groups winning rights for abortion
clinics and doctors; groups demanding rights for white supremacists;
and countless other groups proclaiming the rights for any liberal,
ungodly philosophy or cause imaginable. But don't expect the American
Civil Liberties Union to go to court to fight for rights and special protection of fundamental, Bible-believing Christians. While more than
enough people and groups are pleased to finance and fight for the protection of baby seals, whales, spotted owls, and slimy salamanders, don't
expect anyone to come to the defense of persecuted Christians. Do not
expect anyone to stand up for the rights of those who preach the Bible
and proclaim the gospel of Jesus Christ.

The same people who march and protest for the rights of homosexuals,
abortionists, and endangered animals would gladly hold the coats of the
executioners of Christians and applaud their efforts to silence the church
of Jesus Christ. The current world system is entirely under the dominion of
Satan and is an antichrist world system. "Dear children, this is the last
hour; and as you have heard that the antichrist is coming, even now many
antichrists have come" (1 John 2:18).

America was originally popu-
lated by people attempting to
escape religious persecution in
Europe. They established a society
intentionally designed to protect
and promote gospel-preaching
churches. Nonetheless, this histori-
cal parenthesis of constitutional
protection is rapidly ending. The
constitution has been twisted and

> ❧
>
> *Remember, America was originally populated by men and women attempting to escape religious persecution in Europe.*

distorted and reinterpreted by a liberal, antichrist Supreme Court. The
church and Bible-believing Christians are quickly losing their umbrella of
constitutional protection in the United States. More and more fundamental Christians are seen and depicted as the enemy of a society that is sinking
into moral anarchy.

Conservative evangelical Christians rarely receive positive representa-
tion today. Not in the news media, in movies, or in politics. A church's
benevolent work never makes the news. Local newspapers or television
news stations rarely cover what churches do to reconcile racial divisions
or to provide for the poor or to offer free counseling for the emotionally
distressed or to give care for the sick or to make available community service projects like after-school tutoring or teaching English classes for
immigrants.

It doesn't make the news because it won't get good ratings or bring in
viewers during "sweeps week." It won't sell papers or increase subscrip-
tions. The work of Christian servants and the Christian church rarely
makes news because the work is not this world's work. It is the work of
Christ, this world's perceived enemy. The cameras would rather focus on
the crazy people claiming to be Christians who murder abortion doctors.
They would rather focus on the radical militia movement and somehow tie
it to Christianity. They would rather focus on the David Koreshes and infer,
"This is Christianity, you have to be crazy to be a part of it." Subtly and
slowly, the fundamental, evangelical Christian has been depicted as the
enemy of tolerance and openness. We are now depicted as the enemy of
society. In today's society, everything is tolerated except those who believe

and teach an absolute truth and an absolute God and an absolute salvation through Jesus Christ.

The day could very well be rapidly approaching when we evangelical Christians will be forced once again to live and practice our faith underground. Christians will be hated and openly harassed. We will be prevented from holding public office. We will be required to pay taxes on tithes and offerings. Eventually, churches will be highly regulated by the state. Churches speaking against gay rights and abortion will be closed or silenced by the courts. Imprisonment or litigation awaits pastors speaking on moral issues. We won't be hired as public school teachers or day care workers. We won't be accepted into state universities. Young Christians won't be able to graduate from public schools if they don't meet certain social outcomes of "outcome-based education," including accepting and legitimizing homosexuality. Our children will be taken out of our homes and raised by the state under the jurisdiction of social services if we teach and instill basic biblical values or discipline.

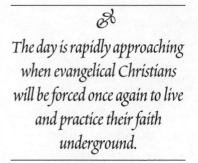

The day is rapidly approaching when evangelical Christians will be forced once again to live and practice their faith underground.

Christians, some day soon, may be called upon once again literally to lay down their lives for Christ. As a believer, follower, and servant of Jesus Christ, you may be the next martyr for Christ. The Lord's servant should expect to face various kinds of suffering:

- "Consider it pure joy, my brothers, whenever you face trials of many kinds" (James 1:2).
- "Many are the afflictions of the righteous" (Ps. 34:19 KJV).
- "In this world you will have trouble" (John 16:33).
- "Now if we are children, then we are heirs—heirs of God and co-heirs with Christ, if indeed we share in his sufferings in order that we may also share in his glory.

"I consider that our present sufferings are not worth comparing with the glory that will be revealed in us" (Rom. 8:17–18).

Your suffering may come in a number of varieties. Never underestimate the creativity of Satan when it comes to finding ways to persecute you. The following list, compiled by Dr. Finnis Drake, details ways you might expect to experience suffering as a servant of Christ:

- Persecution for righteousness (Matt. 5:10; 13:21; Mark 10:30; John 15:20)
- Reviling and slander (Matt. 5:11–12; 10:25; Acts 13:45; 1 Pet. 4:4)
- False accusations (Matt. 10:17–20)
- Scourging for Christ (Matt. 10:17)
- Rejection by others (Matt. 10:14)
- Hatred by the world (Matt. 10:22; John 15:18–21)
- Martyrdom (Matt. 10:28; Acts 7:58)
- Temptation (Luke 8:13; James 1:2–16)
- Shame for his name (Acts 5:41)
- Imprisonment (Acts 4:3; 5:18; 12:4)
- Tribulation (2 Thess. 1:4)
- Stoning (Acts 14:22; 2 Cor. 11:25)
- Beating (Acts 16:22; 2 Cor. 11:24–25)
- Being a spectacle of humanity (1 Cor. 4:9)
- Misunderstandings, necessities, defamation, and despising (1 Cor. 4:10–13)
- Troubles, afflictions, distresses, tumults, labors, watchings, fastings, and evil reports (2 Cor. 6:8–10; 11:26–28)
- Reproaches (Heb. 13:13; 1 Peter 4:14)
- Trials (1 Pet. 1:6; 4:12)
- Satanic opposition (Eph. 4:27; 6:12).[5]

In his book *Freedom of a Christian*, published in 1520, Martin Luther made the statement, "The more Christian a man is, the more evils, sufferings, and deaths he must endure."[6]

We Christians can expect persecution. Even today, you should expect and anticipate subtle forms of persecution. Expect to be harassed and be made fun of for your beliefs. Expect to be turned down for certain jobs and promotions because of your uncompromising positions. Expect to be laughed at and be the victim of jokes by daytime and late night talk show hosts. Expect to see your civil rights slowly erode. Expect to see Christian families harassed by social services and other state agencies. Expect to see your First Amendment right to witness and speak out on moral issues greatly reduced. Expect your tax deductions for charitable contributions soon to be eliminated. Expect to be persecuted as a Christian. Expect this antichrist world system to treat you exactly as it has been treating your spiritual forefathers for twenty centuries. Following Jesus Christ does not come without costs.

Are you still willing to pay the price of servanthood?

Chapter 19

Pain: Purposes and
Prescriptions

∽∽∽

The thought of suffering for Jesus Christ can be intimidating. Much suffering you will experience will be persecution from the world, which hates the new creation you have become. Other suffering, though, will originate from acts of obedient sacrifice. Jesus Christ's servants sacrifice all rights of ownership and hold no possessions. All possessions are God's, and his servants are merely stewards of them. The servant, when deciding to tithe, doesn't ask, "How much of my money will I give to God?" Instead, the servant asks in sacrifice, "How much of God's money will I keep for myself?"

The suffering of voluntary sacrifice goes far beyond money. It is a voluntary sacrifice of one's entire life: career, time and schedule, talents and gifts, personal comforts and conveniences. God may be calling you to sacrifice the comfort and security of family, home, and career and give away your life in ministry. Indeed, you would suffer by way of voluntary sacrifice to sell out and follow God's call into the world. Following Jesus means leaving your dreams, goals, and comforts behind, never looking back. Following Jesus means following him to the cross, where you voluntarily lay down your life in service and surrender.

Beyond sacrificial suffering, we will also suffer the consequences of society's sin. Even though we are Christians, we still live in a fallen world that suffers from all the consequences of sin. Disasters, disease, death, and defeat are all consequences of sin in the world. Even though we are no longer "of the world," we are still "in the world." As a result, we will suffer the consequences of the fall. We will still get sick. We likely will experience financial hardships. We will inevitably be victims of injustices and crimes. We may be victims of natural disasters. We certainly will physically die. Christianity does not exempt us from problems or pain, so expect them to happen. None of us will be totally free from sin's deadly results until Jesus raptures us out of this fallen world of pain and suffering.

Still, the common response to the shock of adversity is, "Why do bad things happen to good people?" The more perplexing question is, "Why do good things always seem to happen to bad people?" Nevertheless, good people ask the original question time and again. They see somebody they love very much, a servant of Jesus, enduring extreme hardship, and the first question they ask is, "Why them?" It just doesn't seem fair.

Don't be surprised when bad things happen to good people. While it is sometimes God's will to heal people in a miraculous way to display his glory, at other times, it's his will to display his glory, grace, and sufficiency through physical suffering.

> *Don't be surprised when bad things happen to good people.*

We see this kind of suffering in Paul, who experienced a "thorn in the flesh." Three times he asked God to heal him. This was the same man who at one time had such a profound spiritual gift of healing that "even handkerchiefs and aprons that touched him were taken to the sick, and their illnesses were cured" (Acts 19:12). Yet God chose not to heal Paul of his own miseries. God received greater glory through Paul's suffering by demonstrating his sufficient grace. "Therefore I will boast all the more gladly about my weaknesses, so that Christ's power may rest on me. That is why, for Christ's sake, I delight in weaknesses, in insults, in hardships, in persecutions, in difficulties. For when I am weak, then I am strong" (2 Cor. 12:9b–10).

Don't be disappointed if God doesn't heal your illness. Look instead for God to be glorified in your suffering as he supplies sufficient grace for whatever pain he may call you to withstand.

Many unbelievers question why bad things happen to good people. Sadly, they come to wrong answers because they don't understand that the source of all suffering is sin. We introduced sin to the world; therefore, suffering and pain are a testimony to our fallen-

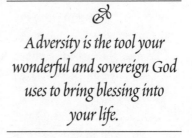

Adversity is the tool your wonderful and sovereign God uses to bring blessing into your life.

ness and depravity. Unbelievers also do not understand God's sovereignty. They don't understand God is so powerful, so wonderful, and so righteous, that he is able to bring good out of the suffering and pain we introduced. Never view adversity and pain as your enemy. Adversity is the tool your wonderful and sovereign God uses to bring blessing into your life. Learn what God is trying to accomplish in your suffering. Learn how to respond to suffering in faith.

Being a Christian will not exempt you from life's hazards. Christians still get in car accidents, become ill, get cancer, suffer heart attacks, or go down in plane crashes. They still lose their jobs or become targets of unjust criticism. If something exists in the world to bring suffering, pain, torment, and misery to the unbeliever, it exists in the world for Christians too.

You may suffer for one other divine reason: discipline. God may decide to discipline you with suffering. Again, Moses appropriately represents the concept of divine discipline (Num. 20:12). He faithfully served God, but he still sinned. When he sinned, he experienced God's divine discipline. When Moses lost his temper, striking the rock to bring water from it as God commanded, he acted in sinful presumption, failing to give God credit and glory. As a result, God told him he would never enter the promised land. When Israel's children came to its border, Moses gave leadership to Joshua and went into the mountains to die.

The Bible teaches,

> "My son, do not make light of the Lord's discipline,
>   and do not lose heart when he rebukes you,
> because the Lord disciplines those he loves,
>   and he punishes everyone he accepts as a son"
> (Heb. 12:5–6).

God's children should not be surprised when they experience hardship from God himself as a means of divine discipline:

> If you are not disciplined (and everyone undergoes discipline), then you are illegitimate children and not true sons. Moreover, we have all had human fathers who disciplined us and we respected them for it. How much more should we submit to the Father of our spirits and live! Our fathers disciplined us for a little while as they thought best; but God disciplines us for our good, that we may share in his holiness. No discipline seems pleasant at the time, but painful. Later on, however, it produces a harvest of righteousness and peace for those who have been trained by it (Heb. 12:8–11).

God's discipline is often painful and difficult, but he disciplines you because he loves you and wants to produce righteousness and holiness in you.

The Bible is filled with examples of God's disciplining his children in love. God disciplined Israel for rebellion, sin, and idolatry. The entire Book of Judges is a repeating cycle of the Israelites' sin—God disciplining them by way of oppressors, the Israelites repenting, and God raising a judge to deliver them from their oppressors. David experienced God's discipline even though he was a man after God's own heart. God disciplined David for committing adultery with Bathsheba with the death of the child born from that sinful relationship. Samson experienced God's discipline with lifelong slavery after Samson prostituted himself, succumbing to his lust for Delilah. The Laodicean church was told to repent of lukewarmness or else God in his wrath would spit them out of his mouth (Rev. 3:16). The Lord said to the church, "Those whom I love I rebuke and discipline" (Rev. 3:19).

There will be times when God brings pain and difficulty into your life to correct you, to chasten you, to awaken you, to cause you to repent of sin, or to drive you to him. This is a sure sign of his intense love for you. Don't buy in

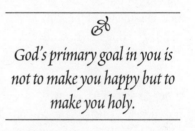

God's primary goal in you is not to make you happy but to make you holy.

on an unbiblical philosophy that says God will never be the initiator of pain or hardship. That line of thinking just doesn't measure up to Scripture. God's primary goal in you is not to make you happy but to make you holy. Sometimes God willingly interrupts your happiness in order to perfect your holiness.

Not all pain comes because of God's discipline. Don't jump to the conclusion that God is punishing you the next time you become ill. When divine discipline is involved, the Holy Spirit will bring with the pain an accompanying deep conviction about a specific sin issue in your life. You'll know when you are receiving divine discipline. In all probability, you will know specifically what God wants to accomplish with it.

Regardless of the origin, the suffering of a servant is always purposeful. God promised to use everything in your life ultimately to bring good to you and to glorify himself. "And we know that in all things God works for the good of those who love him, who have been called according to his purpose" (Rom. 8:28). Suffering will either make you bitter or better, depending on how you respond. Your reaction to adversity and suffering does indeed display the true disposition of your heart.

~

Responding to the Pain

When suffering comes, the first thing you should do is repent of all your known sin. God told the Laodicean church to repent of being so lukewarm. The suffering and discipline they were to endure was meant to drive them to repentance. God may bring hardship into your life in order to deal with sin. Don't rebel against him; repent toward him. Times of suffering and pain in your life should lead you to inspect your life and listen to the convicting ministry of the Holy Spirit. He often will point out some selfish sin that is grieving him and quenching his power in you.

When suffering comes, humble yourself before God. "Humble yourselves, therefore, under God's mighty hand, that he may lift you up in due time" (1 Pet. 5:6). Sometimes God sends adversity because you are too proud, self-sufficient, or self-confident to be the humble servant he wants you to be. For some people, humility comes only through intense and extensive suffering. If we don't learn the lesson God is trying to teach us through adversity, we will have to repeat it until we do learn! Some lessons you will want to learn the first time because you won't want to have to repeat them! Evaluate your personality, disposition, and attitude, asking, "Am I really humble, or am I filled with a lot of pride and self-confidence?" If you find pride in your life, repent and release it, or God will likely move in to take it out of your life.

Next, when suffering comes, obey the command of James 1:2: "Consider it pure joy, my brothers, whenever you face trials of many kinds." You can complain and respond with self-pity or you can respond with a joyful spirit, based on your faith and confidence in God. With your reaction, you have opportunities to witness to the unbelievers around you. You can respond to any and all trials in your life with a spirit of joy because your faith and confidence rest exclusively in the character and control of our great and glorious God. When you complain about inconvenient circumstances and situations in your life, you act like an unbeliever.

When we get caught up in worrying and fretting because of uncertain circumstances in our lives, we are acting just like unbelievers who have no God in whom to depend and trust. Due to our anxiety and stress, we lose our witness before family and friends. Whenever we complain, worry, and fret, we only reveal the true shallowness of our confidence in him. If we truly trust and serve God, then we will respond to adversity with pure joy.

When suffering comes, we are called to give thanks and praise. To give praise and thanks unto the Lord in all circumstances is an act of faith. Paul said, "Give thanks in all circumstances, for this is God's will for you in Christ Jesus" (1 Thess. 5:18). Paul and Silas provide a perfect illustration of this response. At midnight, after having just been brutally beaten and imprisoned in the city of Philippi for preaching the gospel, they lay on their naked backs with their feet in stocks. The Bible asserts that they were "praying and singing hymns to God" (Acts 16:25). They couldn't sleep because of the severe pain in their bodies, so they decided they might as well pray and praise the Lord. Earlier, Peter and the other apostles were brought before the high priest and the Sanhedrin and were strictly commanded to stop preaching the name of Jesus; then they were flogged. "The apostles left the Sanhedrin, rejoicing because they had been counted worthy of suffering disgrace for the Name" (Acts 5:41).

This is our testimony and witness to the world.

Persevere when suffering comes. "Blessed is the man who perseveres under trial, because when he has stood the test, he will receive the crown of life that God has promised to those who love him" (James 1:12). Don't ever quit. You can always tell the measure of a person by what it takes to make that individual quit. God wants you to respond to trials and difficulties in your life with perseverance.

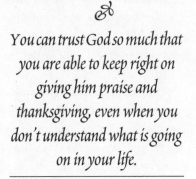

You can trust God so much that you are able to keep right on giving him praise and thanksgiving, even when you don't understand what is going on in your life.

Don't ever let the devil talk you into quitting! Some people get their feelings hurt over the most trivial of issues, and the next thing you know, they're dropping by the wayside. They quit. Self-pity and anger consume them and control their thinking.

Always and above all, when suffering comes, respond in love. Retaliation has no place in a Christian's life. Revenge has no home. Respond in love, just as Christ did on the cross. Paul witnessed to the jailer in Philippi, and that jailer became the first person who was saved in that town (Acts 16). Rely on your spiritual weapons and resources. Your weapons are not the weapons of this world, and you do not do battle the way this world does battle:

> Finally, be strong in the Lord and in his mighty power. Put on the full armor of God so that you can take your stand against the devil's schemes. For our struggle is not against flesh and blood, but against the rulers, against the authorities, against the powers of this dark world and against the spiritual forces of evil in the heavenly realms. Therefore put on the full armor of God, so that when the day of evil comes, you may be able to stand your ground, and after you have done everything, to stand. Stand firm then, with the belt of truth buckled around your waist, with the breastplate

of righteousness in place, and with your feet fitted with the readiness that comes from the gospel of peace. In addition to all this, take up the shield of faith, with which you can extinguish all the flaming arrows of the evil one. Take the helmet of salvation and the sword of the Spirit, which is the word of God. And pray in the Spirit on all occasions with all kinds of prayers and requests. With this in mind, be alert and always keep on praying for all the saints (Eph. 6:10–18).

Our weapons are the weapons of prayer, God's word of truth, fasting, waiting on God, and trusting him. The most effective weapons we have in our battles on earth are the weapons supplied by God. Let God fight your battles. The battle belongs to the Lord:

The weapons we fight with are not the weapons of the world. On the contrary, they have divine power to demolish strongholds. We demolish arguments and every pretension that sets itself up against the knowledge of God, and we take captive every thought to make it obedient to Christ (2 Cor. 10:4–5).

Though the battle is his, you may be called upon to suffer, or even become a casualty. The struggle will be intense. The pain you may feel may burn with tremendous heat. The fire both melts wax and hardens clay. Adversity today will either serve to melt your heart toward God, making you tender and pliable toward him, or it will harden your heart, making you cold, bitter, and resistant toward him. Through it all, God lets you decide how to react to his refining flame. So—break or bend—what will it be?

Chapter 20

The Victories in Suffering

～～～～

Alice Pegues-Miller knows adversity and suffering. She knows all too well the stinging, lingering bite of emotional pain. Not long ago, her husband died. Jim was strong and in good health. She had married the retired Air Force technical sergeant, and they immediately moved across the globe to Turkey. His civil service travels brought them back to the United States, where they relocated in Mississippi. The two were deeply in love and looking forward to many years together. And then he lost his life, succumbing to a fatal heart attack. He was too young to die. He certainly did not fit the demographics of heart attack victims. His death came from nowhere, and losing her husband was painful.

Alice has seen the ugly, scarred appearance of adversity. In her time of mourning, when she searched for explanations, she knew where to go. For though she knew suffering, she also knew God can take the most dreadful, dire circumstances and bring blessing out of them. She didn't look for answers from the world. She found her answers in her Lord and Savior,

Jesus Christ. Alice has said, "When adversity comes knocking at your door, don't be afraid. Take a close look, and you will discover that adversity very well may be a blessing in disguise." Alice knew not to view adversity as her enemy. She looked deep into the worst tragedy of her life and saw God on the other side, supplying sufficient grace and blessing.

Though you may be unable to see God's plan amidst your pain, suffering as a servant of Jesus Christ always brings about victory for his kingdom. God always uses suffering to bring good results. He will use suffering to purify and refine you. Peter revealed the reason for trials and persecutions: "These have come so that your faith—of greater worth than gold, which perishes even though refined by fire—may be proved genuine and may result in praise, glory, and honor when Jesus Christ is revealed" (1 Pet. 1:7).

M. R. DeHaan gave a descriptive analogy of this principle when he said, "A bar of steel worth five dollars is worth ten dollars when made into ordinary horseshoes. If this same five-dollar bar is manufactured into needles, the value rises to $350, but if it is made into delicate springs for expensive watches, it will be worth $250,000. This original bar of steel is made more valuable by being cut to its proper size, passed through the heat again and again, hammered and manipulated, beaten and pounded, finished and polished, until it is finally ready for its delicate task."[7]

God is able to refine your faith and character and shape you into the likeness of Jesus Christ, using every inconvenience and problem you face. When a craftsman polishes a medal, he uses an abrasive material to rub aggressively against it. He will continue polishing and shining until he can see his own reflection in the medal. God works the same way. He is the master craftsman, and you are his medal. Sometimes you will feel God is being a little rough on you. He uses the abrasions of hardship, sickness, and suffering in your life to polish you until he sees his own reflection in you.

> *God is able to refine your faith and character and shape you into the likeness of his Son Jesus Christ, using every inconvenience and problem you face.*

Sometimes it may be difficult to remember God has a master plan far bigger than you. Never think for a moment that God has an ax to grind with you. He instead is allowing you to suffer so that you will discover victory in Christ. God can provide any one of a multitude of victories using suffering as his modus operandi.

Suffering for Greater Glory in Heaven

Paul told the Corinthian church, "For our light and momentary troubles are achieving for us an eternal glory that far outweighs them all" (2 Cor. 4:17). While the body gets weaker during suffering, your spirit is renewed daily. During every moment of your pain and discomfort, Jesus is present. No matter what you endure in this world, no matter how bad it gets, your glory in heaven awaits. God has a home built for you there. Your suffering is not eternal; it will end. Don't lose heart. Give your pain and hurt to God and keep your eyes looking forward to your awaiting glory in the kingdom of Jesus Christ.

> *During every moment of your pain and discomfort, Jesus is present.*

Suffering to Make Jesus Known

A bumper sticker presented the question, "If it were illegal to be a Christian, would there be enough evidence to convict you?" Too many people sidestep suffering for the sake of Christ. These people would rather take the path of least resistance than experience adversity resulting in the proclamation of Jesus Christ's gospel message. Martyrs have dotted the time line of world history with their own blood so that the message of Christ would not be silenced. They willingly suffered in the worst ways, knowing that by doing so, Christ's name would be forever attached to their own testimony, shouting his good news to the world in the process. Be willing to be convicted for your faith in Jesus. By doing so, your testimony of Christ's victory in you may ring through mountains and across oceans.

"For your sake we face death all day long;
we are considered as sheep to be slaughtered" (Rom. 8:36).

Suffering to Bring Life to Others

How we respond to our suffering will be a tremendous testimony to those around us who are unsaved. No doubt our afflictions will pain us. Our pain may seem at times to be unbearable. "For we who are alive are always being given over to death for Jesus' sake, so that his life may be revealed in our mortal body. So then, death is at work in us, but life is at work in you" (2 Cor. 4:11–12). When enduring the pain, we can either curse or praise God. Our words to God will stick with those who do not know him. If an unsaved person can watch us suffer terribly while we continue to thank God for his blessings, ours will be a testimony more powerful than words. Our suffering will be victorious if others come to know their Savior through it.

Suffering to Manifest His Grace

When Paul wrote, "All this is for your benefit, so that the grace that is reaching more and more people may cause thanksgiving to overflow to the glory of God" (2 Cor. 4:15), he fully anticipated a violent death. During the time leading to his death, Paul proclaimed Jesus Christ's grace. He understood that Christ's grace spurred the growth and expansion of Christian faith. He recognized God's presence in the difficulties toward the end of his life, yet he produced overflowing thanks and praise by focusing on the eternal life that lay beyond the grave. Whether or not your suffering is terminal, remember this: God's grace grows faith in the world around you that is far superior to the fading troubles this world causes you to endure.

Suffering to Prepare You to Reign with Christ

You may think you have endured enough suffering to have graduated from the University of Hard Knocks. You may think your suffering should entitle you to be a distinguished professor of pain and misery. If you belong to Christ, though, you can take solace in knowing, "If we endure, we will also reign with him" (2 Tim. 2:12).

> *If you belong to Jesus Christ, you can take solace in the knowledge that your suffering is teaching you how to reign with Christ.*

Your suffering teaches you how to reign with Christ. As his servant, you should seek to go wherever God is calling you, even if you will suffer by following his will. When you acknowledge Christ before the world in the most adverse situations and conditions, he will acknowledge you before his Father in heaven.

Suffering to Bring Glory to Himself

In John's Gospel, Jesus and his disciples came to a man who had been blind from birth. Christ's disciples asked, "Rabbi, who sinned, this man or his parents, that he was born blind?" (John 9:1). Jesus answered, "Neither this man nor his parents sinned . . . but this happened so that the work of God might be displayed in his life" (John 9:3). Jesus then miraculously healed the blind man. Later, Jesus was given news his dear friend Lazarus was sick and dying. "When he heard this, Jesus said, 'This sickness will not end in death. No, it is for God's glory so that God's Son may be glorified through it'" (John 11:4). Jesus waited four days to go to Bethany. But when he got there, he performed the greatest of all his miracles. He raised Lazarus from the dead. At times, God will allow you to face impossible situations as an opportunity for him to display his miraculous power. After raising Lazarus, many of the Jews who witnessed the event came to put their faith in Christ. Maybe God is using you to show his power so that those around you will do the same.

~

Suffering to Teach You Humility

Paul said God had given him a thorn in the flesh to "keep [him] from becoming conceited because of these surpassingly great revelations, there was given [him] a thorn in [his] flesh" (2 Cor. 12:7). All Christians occasionally get "too big for their britches." Even Christians can gain a sense of invincibility when they experience nothing but blessings and successes. Human nature causes us to forget God when our paths are lined with rose petals and good-luck pennies. When we forget about God and start giving ourselves the credit for the blessings in our lives, we have forgotten to serve him. Jesus said, "I am the vine; you are the branches. If a man remains in me, and I in him, he will bear much fruit; apart from me you can do nothing" (John 15:5). Perhaps God allows a hardship to come just to reduce the swelling in the head filled with pride.

~

Suffering to Teach Dependence on Him

God knows when you grow self-sufficient. To drive you to himself and to teach you to depend totally upon him, God may periodically send adversity your way. Paul said, "But he said to me, 'My grace is sufficient for you, for my power is made perfect in weakness.' Therefore I will boast all the more gladly about my weaknesses, so that Christ's power may rest on me. That is why, for Christ's sake, I delight in weaknesses, in insults, in hardships, in persecutions, in difficulties. For when I am weak, then I am strong" (2 Cor. 12:9–10).

~

Suffering to Teach Patience and Perseverance

When you suffer, your world stops. You quit going to power lunches and start going to the hospital. You quit giving counsel, and

Suffering moves you from the "fast lane," steering right toward the "faith lane."

you start seeking it. You stop making things happen, and you start letting things happen. Suffering moves you from the "fast lane," steering right toward the "faith lane." You slow down. You let God "drive" your life. You become patient. You wait upon him. You persevere. You trust him. You mature. You "consider it pure joy, my brothers, whenever you face trials of many kinds, because you know that the testing of your faith develops perseverance. Perseverance must finish its work so that you may be mature and complete, not lacking anything" (James 1:2–4). You become complete, experiencing victory in Jesus Christ.

Suffering to Develop Your Spiritual Maturity

Driving through the rolling hills of a countryside, you will notice the natural phenomenon—grass grows thicker and greener in valleys than on mountaintops. God will allow us to go through some valley experiences in life in order to grow us. "No discipline seems

> *God will allow you to go through some "valley experiences" in life in order to grow you.*

pleasant at the time, but painful. Later on, however, it produces a harvest of righteousness and peace for those who have been trained by it" (Heb. 12:11). God has no intention of treating us like the child who is left to himself and never disciplined and grows up physically but not emotionally. That child grows to be a very immature adult. God knows he must discipline us in order to help us mature spiritually. God knows suffering will drive us to him, to his Word, to prayer. The experience will grow, develop, and mature us.

Victories in suffering—the connection is a paradox. This concept comes from the same Jesus who said that to be first you must be last. Remember, he is the only king ever to give his entire life over to serving his people. Only his concepts all come together and bring victory. Jesus planned victories for you and the world. When you suffer, don't fret. Don't curse.

Rejoice! Victory awaits!

Part Six:

The Servant Evangelist

Chapter 21

Philip: Servant and Evangelist

꙳꙳꙳

On a piece of paper, write the names of people you know who are not Christians. First write names of family who do not know Jesus. Next, add names of friends, both new and old. Next, add names of persons with whom you interact in business. Then add names of those with whom you have casual contact. Add names of families in the neighborhood, the person who delivers your mail, and the ones who collect your garbage. Before you put your pen down and continue reading, think again. Finally, add names of people you may have met in passing. Think of those to whom you have been introduced at parties. Write down the name of the guy telling the dirty joke. Write down the names of the people laughing hysterically at his well-timed punch line. If you can't quite put your finger on the name, just write down enough description to remind you of the face. God knows who you are thinking of. Keep writing and thinking until you feel satisfied you've written down the names or descriptions of all the people you know who don't know Jesus Christ as their personal Savior.

Your page should be filled with names. When you see these names, you should see their faces. Looking at the names, memories likely swirl through your brain. You likely remember times that make you joyously laugh, happily smile, or maybe poignantly brim with teary longings. These are names of people you know, love, and respect. You can visualize the work they do with or for you. In some cases, you can see their families. (Did you remember to include their names on the list?) These are people who complete your world. Can you visualize that they are destined for hell? Can you see that every one of them will be eternally tormented with separation from their loving God and Savior? If you know these people are not saved, hell is the eternal destination for each and every one of the names on your list.

Do you ever pray for these people? Do you have a real passion to see them come to know Christ as their Savior? Do you ever wish someone would talk to them about Christ and somehow encourage them to surrender their lives to the Lord? Did the thought ever occur to you that maybe you are the one God

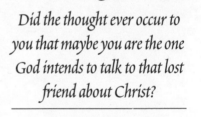

Did the thought ever occur to you that maybe you are the one God intends to talk to that lost friend about Christ?

intends to talk to that lost friend about Christ? Maybe it was no accident that God placed you in that person's life. Possibly, God's design orchestrated you to know that person. His reason for uniting you may be so you can tell that lost person about Jesus. You may be the only Bible the lost person will ever read. You may be the only Jesus the lost person will ever see. You may be the only one who can talk to the lost person about Christ. While your circle of unsaved friends may be quite large, it is very likely that the lost person's circle of saved friends is quite small.

What exactly keeps you from sharing Christ? What is stopping you from attempting to witness to the people whose names are staring at you from the paper in your hands? Are you afraid of the unknown? You don't know what they'll think of you if you step out and preach Jesus. You don't know how they'll react or respond. You might offend them. You might say something that will cause them to steer clear of you. You might look silly. You might sound awkward. You might hurt your own reputation. You might drive them away.

Those names on your list are already headed for hell. You may be the last sentry on a lonely road. You may be the last voice they'll hear, shouting to them that the bridge has been washed out, that only eternal death lies ahead and it is time to turn around right now. If you remain silent out of fear or apprehension, you may be muzzling the only mouth knowing the eternal difference Jesus Christ makes.

It is normal to have inhibitions when it comes to spreading the gospel. I, a preacher and pastor, have the very same fears when it comes to talking to my family, friends, and acquaintances about Jesus Christ, and I am a "paid professional." John Kramp wrote: "The one thing upon which Christians and non-Christians agree is that they both dislike evangelism. The very word conjures up 'in your face' confrontations. Therefore, Christians usually avoid gospel showdowns and most non-Christians are relieved they do!"[8]

Like it or not, when you become a servant, you become an evangelist. The word *evangelist* in today's world lugs heavy bags of negative connotation. Evangelist conjures an image of some guy with tall, slicked-back hair and gold rings covering eight out of ten fingers like small, misplaced paperweights. You see this man with ten suits and ten sermons riding a road show. He comes into your town and puts on a dog and pony show to try to "evangelize." In your mind's eye, you might also see a TV personality and his wife. He wears more gold than the traveling evangelist and somehow is able to stretch the word *God* into four syllables. She looks like her hair was styled by a Kansas tornado and wears enough makeup to pass for a circus clown. Across the television screen, they flash their overly white, capped teeth in large smiles, pleading with you to come to Jesus. By the way, as tears flow on their faces through thick makeup causing mud-slides, they ask you to send all the money you can. They want to sell you a miracle for money.

These people are charlatans, not evangelists. *Evangelism* is not a synonym for *fraud*. An *evangelist* is defined as "one who bears good news." Translated the word *evangelize* (*euaggalizo*) simply means "good news."

> ❧
>
> *Every person who knows and has experienced the truth about Jesus Christ is a bearer of good news.*

Every person who has been born again and knows Jesus Christ personally is an evangelist. Every person who knows and has experienced the truth about Jesus Christ is a bearer of good news. The church has a specific office of evangelist because the Scriptures clearly teach God gave some to be apostles, some to be prophets, some to be evangelists, and some to be pastors and teachers. The office of evangelist is set aside for those with a special calling and giftedness in evangelizing.

Though some are particularly called to the position, the ministry of witnessing and sharing the good news of Jesus Christ is a ministry all Christians share. All Christians share the privilege and responsibility. You have been called to be an evangelist. The Bible shares a story about one man who took the ministry of evangelism very seriously:

> And the angel of the Lord spake unto Philip, saying, Arise, and go toward the south unto the way that goeth down from Jerusalem unto Gaza, which is desert. And he arose and went: and, behold, a man of Ethiopia, an eunuch of great authority under Candace queen of the Ethiopians, who had the charge of all her treasure, and had come to Jerusalem for to worship, Was returning, and sitting in his chariot read Esaias the prophet. Then the Spirit said unto Philip, Go near, and join thyself to this chariot. And Philip ran thither to him, and heard him read the prophet Esaias, and said, Understandest thou what thou readest? And he said, How can I, except some man should guide me? And he desired Philip that he would come up and sit with him. The place of the scripture which he read was this, He was led as a sheep to the slaughter; and like a lamb dumb

before his shearer, so opened he not his mouth: In his humiliation his judgment was taken away: and who shall declare his generation? for his life is taken from the earth. And the eunuch answered Philip, and said, I pray thee, of whom speaketh the prophet this? of himself, or of some other man? Then Philip opened his mouth, and began at the same scripture, and preached unto him Jesus. And as they went on their way, they came unto a certain water: and the eunuch said, See, here is water; what doth hinder me to be baptized? And Philip said, If thou believest with all thine heart, thou mayest. And he answered and said, I believe that Jesus Christ is the Son of God. And he commanded the chariot to stand still: and they went down both into the water, both Philip and the eunuch; and he baptized him. And when they were come up out of the water, the Spirit of the Lord caught away Philip, that the eunuch saw him no more: and he went on his way rejoicing. But Philip was found at Azotus: and passing through he preached in all the cities, till he came to Caesarea (Acts 8:26–40 KJV).

Philip is one of the Bible's best examples of a servant evangelist. This look at a small slice of his life reveals he was equally concerned with each part of his unofficial title, spending time as a servant and an evangelist.

> *Philip is one of the best examples in all the Bible of what it means to be an evangelist.*

Philip the Servant

The first controversy arising in the early church is recorded in Acts 6. The church operated in a day when the government never offered social security and had no federal welfare plan. The church ministered to its widows, caring for those who had no income. This vital part of the early church's ministry was embroiled in controversy. The church at Jerusalem had members who were converted Jews from Jerusalem as well as Jews and

Gentiles who had lived most of their lives in some other part of the Roman Empire. These latter Jews were called "Grecian Jews" because they were more culturally Greek and Roman than they were Jew. As the church grew rapidly, the Grecian Jews felt their widows were neglected by the apostles' widow-care ministry, so they registered a complaint. The apostles had not intentionally neglected the Grecian widows. The church simply grew so fast that they could not keep up with all the necessary ministry.

The apostles decided it was time to prioritize the many ministries of the church. They delegated work, asking the church to choose seven men who could lead the widows' food distribution ministry, so the apostles could focus on their ministry of the word and prayer:

> In those days when the number of disciples was increasing, the Grecian Jews among them complained against the Hebraic Jews because their widows were being overlooked in the daily distribution of food. So the Twelve gathered all the disciples together and said, "It would not be right for us to neglect the ministry of the word of God in order to wait on tables. Brothers, choose seven men from among you who are known to be full of the Spirit and wisdom. We will turn this responsibility over to them and will give our attention to prayer and the ministry of the word."

> This proposal pleased the whole group. They chose Stephen, a man full of faith and of the Holy Spirit; also Philip, Procorus, Nicanor, Timon, Parmenas, and Nicolas from Antioch, a convert to Judaism. They presented these men to the apostles, who prayed and laid their hands on them.

> So the word of God spread. The number of disciples in Jerusalem increased rapidly, and a large number of priests became obedient to the faith (Acts 6:1–7).

Most Bible scholars agree that these seven, including Philip, were the first deacon servants chosen by the church. Philip was chosen to take responsibility for distributing food to the widows. His nomination reveals he must have been recognized for being full of the Spirit and wisdom. He must have been recognized as having a servant's heart.

Philip the Evangelist

Philip is later shown living in his hometown of Caesarea, raising four godly daughters who possessed the spiritual gift of prophecy. He was still a faithful witness. By the time Paul stopped and spent time at his house, Philip had a strong reputation as an evangelist:

> We continued our voyage from Tyre and landed at Ptolemais, where we greeted the brothers and stayed with them for a day. Leaving the next day, we reached Caesarea and stayed at the house of Philip the evangelist, one of the Seven. He had four unmarried daughters who prophesied (Acts 21:7–9).

Philip was just a layman who truly loved Jesus. He was filled with the Spirit. He was not highly educated. He had no seminary training. He wasn't a pastor. He wasn't an apostle. He was an average, normal guy. Philip demonstrated you don't need a string of theological degrees to bear testimony of Jesus Christ and lead people to faith in him. You

Philip demonstrated you don't need a string of theological degrees to bear testimony of Jesus Christ and lead people to faith in him.

should take advantage of training made available to you, but it is not essential. The only thing you need to witness effectively is your own personal testimony of how you came to Christ. Philip was just like you. You can be just like him. You can be a servant. You can be an evangelist. Being a servant and an evangelist naturally go hand in hand. You cannot accurately call yourself a servant until you are actively evangelizing. You can be a servant evangelist.

Chapter 22

Lost in the Wilderness

୬ଡ଼୬ଡ଼୬

I peered north from the apex of the craggy peak. The sun had yet to awaken. Wild grass, brown from the chill of autumn, sagged with a heavy coat of Colorado Rocky Mountain dew. I, along with Ralph Eberhardt, a friend and deacon at Riverside, had passed the tree line as though it were little more than a checkpoint on an important exploration. We were scouting the land, surveying it for the prospects it might bring during hunting season. We had parked our vehicle on a rugged, rutted road and trudged up a particularly promising ridge line to the peak where I stood. The view was breathtaking. We could see well into the thick brush. We could see the trails the deer and elk used as escape routes. We saw their bedding areas and watering holes. Atop this Colorado mountain peak, we could see all the way to Wyoming in one direction and to Utah in another. We could also see the fog rolling up the side of the mountain like an unfurling ashen gray carpet.

The climb had taken more than half an hour. In less than a minute, my friend and I were swallowed by the fog and could not see fifty feet in any direction. Utah and Wyoming were only distant memories. We had lost all visible reference points. We began to backtrack, or so we hoped. Nothing looked familiar. We wandered for two hours, trying to locate the original ridge line that had led us to the peak. I held a compass, but it may as well have been a road map. Its directional assistance could not identify the exact ridge leading to our truck. Anxiety tapped a bony finger of discontent upon my shoulder as the disorientation grew more profound. I began looking for the safest place to "hole up" for the night while I looked for the ridge.

All the while we searched, we knew only one thing for certain: we did not want to withstand the shame and embarrassment of needing an alpine rescue team to save us. I thought I just might decide to stay lost rather than face the humiliation of being brought back by rangers to face our fellow campers. As hope faded, the fog momentarily lifted. I looked up and discovered I was standing on the original ridge. We finally made our way down to the hunting camp two hours late, where only a few small truth distortions saved us from humiliation and teasing that would have come if the other men had known what really happened.

Our world is filled with people who bumble aimlessly in a spiritual fog. Most don't realize they're lost. Many are having fun. No one gets lost on purpose. Few admit they are lost. Some are just beginning to realize they are lost, and they are frightened. Others are calling out into the fog, looking and grasping for anything to give them a sense of direction.

Only Christians make up the spiritual "alpine rescue team." We are the only rescue team prepared to lead lost people home safely. We have to be willing to go and find the lost. We must be like Jesus, who "came to seek and save [those who are] lost" (Luke 19:10).

You cannot honestly define yourself as Christ's servant until you feel the same way he feels about lost people and you adopt his mission to "seek and save" lost people. The church's mission and commission is the same today as it was two thousand years ago when Jesus originally gave it:

> Therefore go and make disciples of all nations, baptizing them
> in the name of the Father and of the Son and of the Holy Spirit,

and teaching them to obey everything I have commanded you. And surely I am with you always, to the very end of the age (Matt. 28:19–20).

Even though God's command to evangelize is clear, many Christians feel no compelling reason to evangelize. The problem most Christians have is they have forgotten how it feels to be lost. The longer you live as a Christian, the more likely it is you have moved away from most or all of your pre-Christian friends. You have lost contact with that world. You have adopted a new lifestyle and have forgotten how it feels to be lost.

Philip never forgot what it was like to be lost. He remembered so well how it felt to be lost that it drove him to constant evangelism. His memories of fear, disorientation, and uneasiness led him to search out the lost and lead them to the Savior. The Ethiopian eunuch of Acts 8:26–40 was one of those he led to Christ. Just before the two met, the Ethiopian realized he was lost and needed somebody to point the way for him. In verse 30, Philip ran up to the chariot and heard this man reading aloud (customary in that day) from the Book of Isaiah. He was reading from Isaiah 53, a strong Messianic prophecy of Christ's substitutionary death. Philip asked him, "Do you understand what you are reading?"

The eunuch's reply sends a powerful message to those who are not convinced that all Christians are evangelists. He answered, "How can I, except some man should guide me?" (Acts 8:31 KJV).

The Heart of a Servant Evangelist

Philip's response to God as well as to the Ethiopian provides tremendous insight to the heart of this servant evangelist. Remember, he was just like you, and you can be just like him. He was never inhibited by prejudice. The person Philip met and climbed into the chariot with to witness about Jesus Christ was "a man of Ethiopia, an eunuch of great authority under Candace queen of Ethiopians, who had the charge of all her treasure" (Acts 8:27 KJV).

Any one of many social barriers could have clouded Philip's heart with prejudice. Race was an obvious barrier. The Ethiopian was black. If Philip had been raised in today's typical church, he might not have run to witness to him. There was also a sexual barrier. The Ethiopian was an emasculated eunuch. For obvious reasons, royal court officials who had charge over the king's harem were often emasculated. Under Jewish law, there was a great prejudice toward castrated men. Even though this man had been to Jerusalem to worship, he could never be considered a full or complete Jew. According to the law in Deuteronomy 23:1, he could become a "God fearer" or a "proselyte of the gate," but he could never become a full Jew because of his emasculation. Philip could have very easily said, "If this guy can't be a full Jew, he probably can't be a full Christian either. I don't think I'll waste my time with him."

Philip never said that. He witnessed to him. Philip wasn't blinded by prejudice. If you are a true servant evangelist, your heart cannot be clouded by any prejudice. Jesus commanded us to disciple "all nations." All nations comes from the Greek word *ethnos,* the root of the English word *ethnic.* The word literally means "all ethnic groups." The gospel is for everyone. It is for blacks as well as whites. It is for the poor as well as the rich. It is for Asians as well as Americans. Prejudices do not exist with Jesus Christ. He is the Savior of the entire world.

> *If you are going to be a true servant evangelist, you cannot have your heart clouded by prejudice of any kind.*

Philip was not easily intimidated. Position or power meant little to him. The eunuch he ran toward was important. He was a member of the queen's cabinet. He was a foreign ambassador, a dignitary. The Ethiopian was the chief treasurer of the Ethiopian government. He was the finance minister, the treasury secretary. He was important! You can be certain his importance was obvious. No doubt the chariot he rode in was obviously an ornate chariot of true royalty. He probably traveled with a large entourage of aides and associates. Meanwhile, Philip was just a common Joe. He was average, run of the mill. He was a commoner. If you had been Philip, it could have been intimidating to be told by the Lord to go witness to this wealthy, powerful ambassador from another country.

It takes courage to witness to someone in a position of power or authority over you. It's tough to witness to someone wealthier than you. It can be hard to witness to your teacher or professor, a boss, supervisor, CEO, coach, to someone wealthy or famous, or to your senator or congressman. The thought can be intimidating until you remember, "Greater is he that is in you, than he that is in the world" (1 John 4:4 KJV), and "I can do all things through Christ which strengtheneth me" (Phil. 4:13 KJV).

You don't ever have to be intimidated about witnessing to anyone. You are the "light of the world" and light always conquers darkness. Christ has promised always to be with you when you witness and share, declaring, "At that time you will be given what to say, for it will not be you speaking, but the Spirit of your Father speaking through you" (Matt. 10:19). He has promised to give you exactly the words you need, if you will depend on him.

The Availability of the Evangelist

God does not need your ability. He needs only your availability. Philip's ability did not make him a powerful servant evangelist. His simple, humble, spontaneous availability is what made him such

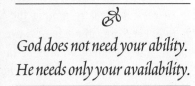

God does not need your ability. He needs only your availability.

a powerful servant evangelist. When the angel of the Lord confronted him, he was preaching a very successful evangelistic crusade in Samaria. Suddenly, God asked Philip to leave all the successful ministry to the Samarian masses to go down a desert road leading to a "nowhere" land called Gaza. Just when things were really beginning to happen in Samaria, Philip pulled up stakes and jumped ship right in the middle of the revival. If Philip were an evangelist under today's understanding of the job, this action would be hard on his reputation. Philip was not concerned about his reputation. For him, his reputation as an evangelist took a backseat to his obedience. When an angel told him to take a road trip, he did it. He was more concerned with being a true servant.

Have you ever made yourself totally available to the Lord, without regard to what it may do to your reputation? Worries about what other people will think about you may be stopping you. As long as you are worried about what other people are thinking, you cannot possibly be totally available to the Lord. You cannot serve yourself and serve the Lord at the same time. To be available to God means you quit worrying about your own reputation.

Also, Philip was not concerned about results. He understood a very basic principle about Christian life and witnessing: his responsibility was simply to obey God and leave the results to him. Successful witnessing means sharing Christ in the power of the Holy Spirit and leaving the results to God. Understanding this principle will help you realize you can never be a failure in witnessing if you are sharing Christ in the power of the Holy Spirit. Whether or not the person responds by receiving Christ as Savior at that moment does not matter.

You are not responsible for the results. God is.

Philip did not need assurance of any results when God told him to leave his successful ministry among the Samaritans to hike into the desert. Philip obeyed him immediately, even though God gave no assurance of what he intended to do with Philip on the dusty road. Philip's instructions from the angel were scant. God did not tell him the how, when, and where behind his command to go. God simply said, "Go to Gaza." Philip didn't ask, "Why, Lord?" He just went.

Even after Philip spotted the chariot, he didn't know what he was supposed to be doing. Once again, God gave instructions, though he revealed no purpose or intent. "The Spirit told Philip, 'Go to that chariot and stay near it'" (Acts 8:29). If Philip were a modern evangelist, he would likely have complained to the Lord. He might have said, "Lord, this is crazy. I left a perfectly good ministry up in Samaria. I had a nice motel room there. I've been walking for almost two days now. It's hot. I'm hungry. My bunions are killing me. My sandals have worn a blister on my feet. Now you tell me to run up to that chariot and try to stay near it. Who do you think I am . . . Carl Lewis? Tell that guy to park that thing. Then I'll talk to him."

Thankfully, Philip was a true servant evangelist. The Bible says, "Then Philip ran up to the chariot" (Acts 8:30). The whole time, Philip never knew God's plan. He just knew he needed to make himself available to God, no matter what God wanted. If you simply make yourself available to God, you don't have to find witnessing opportunities. God will set them up for you.

Finally, Philip was not concerned about the risks. God did not tell Philip to take the best route to Gaza. He told Philip to take the lesser traveled of two roads leading from Jerusalem to Gaza, a "desert road"(Acts 8:26). There was no water. This road was filled with thieves and robbers. It was a big risk for a person to travel this road alone. Philip gave no thought to his own personal well-being or the possible risks involved with such an assignment, because Philip was available to God.

> *If you simply make yourself available to God, you don't have to go looking for witnessing opportunities. God will set them up for you.*

Most people today don't witness more often because they don't want to take the personal risks it involves. We don't want to risk our reputation. We don't want to risk our image. We don't want to risk humiliation. We don't want to risk the possible repercussion. You may risk losing your job if you witness to someone at the local school where you teach or the agency where you work. You will never be an effective witness until you are willing to be fully available to him, no matter what the risks may be to you personally.

Look again at that list of names you compiled. Those people are still the same. Some don't know they are lost. Others know and are calling out for someone to lead them to the Savior. Some have been lost for so long they have forgotten they are lost. None of them meant to lose their way; it was just their nature. Whether they realize it or not, all of them are hoping for a servant evangelist to find them. You may be their only hope. You may be the only servant evangelist they ever have the chance to know. Now is the time to pick up the Word of God and go. Make a life-saving rescue.

Chapter 23

Under Conviction

∽∾∽

Before you were saved, the Holy Spirit convicted you of the truth of God's plan and God's love for you. You may have tried to reason your way out of salvation or you may have tried to deny the message. You may have fought the Holy Spirit, foolishly holding onto the worldly habits and ways you had grown to love and were reluctant to give up for the sake of Jesus Christ. In the end, though, you relented to the truth of the Holy Spirit. His conviction was undeniable and irrefutable. When you saw the truth, you obeyed, and you were saved.

Even though your eternal destination is assured, the Holy Spirit continues to convict. He lives in you daily, helping you resist temptation, giving you wisdom to do the things that Christ would do. The Holy Spirit provides your plumb line of truth. When you stray, he convicts you of your wandering.

You need to know that sharing the gospel message of Jesus Christ to the world around you is not an option. Witnessing is your responsibility.

Christ called you to be a servant and an evangelist, so perhaps it is time to quit running around in religious circles. In the four Gospels, you see that Jesus ran around with the nonreligious and the unsaved. Follow the example set by your Savior, and be his representative on earth to the unsaved. Be that plumb line of truth to those around you. Let your life be such that it convicts others that Christ is the one necessary ingredient they lack. Remember your responsibility as a servant and evangelist.

The danger of forgetting your responsibilities is that you quit listening to the Holy Spirit's convicting direction. You begin listening to the world. You buy into a concept of universalism, which suggests that all New Agers, Hindus, Buddhists, even atheists will go to heaven because no loving God would condemn his children to hell. You begin to think your path to God is assured, but so are the paths of others, even though they do not have a saving relationship with Jesus Christ. You may begin to think the road to heaven is a multilane superhighway. You accept lifestyle choices because you don't want to be labeled as being judgmental. You forget to stand firm for your faith, for the truth, and for your God.

The Bible responds to fallacious beliefs sternly and without ground for discussion or disagreement. The Bible says the only way to heaven is through a loving, personal relationship with Jesus Christ. If a person, any person, dies outside of a relationship with Jesus Christ, that person is sent immediately, irrevocably, and eternally to a place of eternal torment called hell. Whether you want to believe it or

> *If a person, any person, dies outside of a relationship with Jesus Christ, that person is sent immediately, irrevocably, and eternally to a place of eternal torment called hell.*

not, your family members, your friends, and your acquaintances will go to hell if they die without that relationship with Jesus Christ. If they die before you take the opportunity to witness to them, you will have lost your chance to do what you can to keep them from that terrible destination.

That's the truth.

The good news is God loves us so much that he provides the one and only way to salvation from that destination. Jesus Christ is the salvation for your family, friends, and acquaintances. Jesus is not *a* way, *a* truth, or *a* life. He is *the* way, *the* truth, and *the* life. The world may call you narrow-minded and bigoted, but Jesus Christ himself said, "No one comes to the Father except through me" (John 14:6). Either Jesus Christ is the only way, or he is no way at all. The testimony of those who believe, both living and those long since deceased, affirm through the Word and through experience that he is, indeed, the only way.

Follow the Leader

The same Holy Spirit who convicted you to accept salvation and who convicts you to witness to those around you will tell you when, where, and how you should actively evangelize and witness. He will prepare you and the person(s) with whom you will interact. Never forget, God is in control. He is working with you and them to bring the greatest good for his glory. The Holy Spirit is busy preparing right now.

The Holy Spirit was at work in the meeting between Philip and the Ethiopian. He made the arrangements and set up the appointment. He convicted the Ethiopian and Philip of separate truths. Both obeyed, and a life was won for the kingdom of Christ.

The Holy Spirit prepared the Ethiopian. None of the details creating the meeting between him and Philip could have happened by mere accident or coincidence. The Holy Spirit sovereignly coordinated everything. It was no accident that the Ethiopian had been in Jerusalem to worship at this time. It was no accident that the Ethiopian was on the road to Gaza, in this particular spot at this particular time. It was no accident that the Ethiopian and Philip met on this road in the middle of nowhere. It was no accident that the Ethiopian was reading from the Old Testament, in particular the fifty-third chapter of the prophet Isaiah, which speaks specifically of Christ's vicarious suffering and atonement. It was no accident that Philip was on the road at the same time. It was no accident that Philip was the disciple who met the Ethiopian, because he was a Hellenistic Jew and more open to people of different cultures.

From a purely human perspective, the chances that all these pieces would happen at just the right time and fall together perfectly are absurdly outlandish. The chances are so astronomically unlikely, they defy any imaginable probability or possibility. The chances that Philip would meet up with the chariot on that long stretch of barren road are transparently slim. The chances that their paths would cross at just the precise time the Ethiopian was reading from Isaiah 53 are realistically impossible. Only the loving, active work of the Holy Spirit could plan it so well.

When Philip approached the chariot and heard the man reading aloud about Christ Jesus suffering as the Lamb of God, Philip started to get excited. He knew then why God had sent him on this crazy mission way out in no-man's-land. God had been preparing the heart of this Ethiopian. God had put a hunger in his heart for the Lord. It is the only way to explain why he traveled the perilous two-hundred-plus miles from his home to Jerusalem. God had caused his hunger to be unsatisfied by the dry, formal, lifeless worship of the Jewish temple. God had arranged for him to be reading from this powerful passage in Isaiah 53. God had stirred a passion in his heart to understand what the passage meant. By the time Philip arrived, most of the work had been done. The Ethiopian was ready to trust Jesus. The Holy Spirit had prepared the Ethiopian's heart. Philip didn't have to do much of anything except to explain to him the truth about Jesus. You could have done what Philip did!

The Holy Spirit prompted Philip to go to the Ethiopian. The Lord told Philip to leave Samaria and head to Gaza. The Lord did all the prompting in Philip's heart. On that barren road, the Ethiopian was spiritually hungry, and Philip was spiritually available.

When you have a spiritually hungry person meet with a spiritually available servant evangelist, you have a divine appointment. Somebody is going to get saved. The Holy Spirit is working in people's lives, just as he did with the Ethiopian. The Holy Spirit is also attempting to prepare you to be the verbal witness people need. If you yield yourself to become an available witness, it won't be long before you discover a whole community of interested people around you. You will see that God has been working in people's lives where you work, shop, go to school, and live. You will discover that God is working in many people's lives. Now he is prompting you to be a Philip to these people.

God is at work in people's lives around you in a million different ways. He uses circumstances and people to prepare those around you, just like he did this Ethiopian. If you will be sensitive and available to the Holy Spirit, you won't have to force your witness on them. You won't have to beat people over the

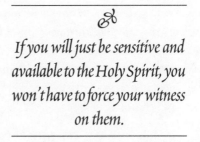

If you will just be sensitive and available to the Holy Spirit, you won't have to force your witness on them.

head with a Bible. You won't have to cram Scripture down their throats. You won't have to drag them to church kicking and screaming. Be available and sensitive and alert. God will lead you to people who are open and receptive and ready to receive a witness from you about Jesus Christ.

You can be an effective witness and evangelist. You don't have to have a degree in theology or have high-level training. You don't have to have the entire New Testament memorized to be effective. The message is not about theology, philosophy, or church doctrine. The message is about Jesus Christ!

Don't replace the message of Jesus with other, nonessential matters. For instance, it is good to talk to people about your church and even invite them to the service, but this isn't real evangelism. The message of evangelism is Jesus! While it is good to discuss doctrinal differences between churches, it is not evangelism. Evangelism is Jesus! And it is good to talk to people about church, but it is not evangelism. The equation is simple. Evangelism = Jesus!

You might assume that if you invite somebody to church, you have done your evangelism work for the day. That may not be enough. What if the person doesn't hear the message for whatever reason? Continue to invite as many people to church as you can, but know that the church can never displace or substitute the real message of evangelism, which is to have a loving relationship with Jesus Christ. The ultimate mission is to help people face the Savior and put their faith in him. If you are a born-again Christian, you can tell people about Jesus Christ. If you can remember how you became a Christian, you can tell others how to do it too. Be like

Philip, who, "began with that very passage of Scripture and told him the good news about Jesus" (Acts 8:35).

Do you want to become an evangelist? Just open your mouth and tell people about Jesus. Most people don't want to hear about more "religion." A lot of them already have had bad experiences with organized religion. Most, though, will be very willing to have an open discussion about the living person of Jesus Christ. They will be willing to talk about Jesus.

You Have to Follow Through

Follow-through is an important concept in life. In sports, you need proper follow-through to bowl strikes, throw strikes, or have the perfect golf swing. In business, follow-through is the art of closing the deal or the method of good customer service. In relationships, follow-through is how you show you care or how you make sure you've thought of everything. In evangelism, follow-through is equally essential.

Philip followed through with leading the Ethiopian to placing his complete faith and trust in Jesus Christ:

> And as they went on their way, they came unto a certain water: and the eunuch said, See, here is water; what doth hinder me to be baptized? And Philip said, If thou believest with all thine heart, thou mayest. And he answered and said, I believe that Jesus Christ is the Son of God. And he commanded the chariot to stand still: and they went down both into the water, both Philip and the eunuch; and he baptized him. And when they were come up out of the water, the Spirit of the Lord caught away Philip, that the eunuch saw him no more: and he went on his way rejoicing (Acts 8:36–39 KJV).

The follow-through of the evangelist involves baptism. The Ethiopian desired to be baptized. Baptism should be the immediate desire of every person who puts his faith and trust in Jesus Christ. Once Philip knew the Ethiopian was trusting in Christ completely, he made no other requirement of him to be baptized. This example fits the biblical pattern. Don't expect people to reach some point of spiritual discipleship or maturity before baptism. Baptism is an important step of obedience toward maturity and spiritual discipleship.

Philip's baptism of the Ethiopian shows that baptism is for believers only. Unbelievers are not to be baptized, nor are people who are unable to make their own personal, cognizant decision regarding Jesus Christ. Babies aren't ready for baptism; the practice of infant baptism did not begin until three hundred years after Christ's resurrection. Philip told the Ethiopian that the one and only prerequisite for baptism was that he make a full commitment of faith in Jesus Christ. The order in which you are baptized is essential. If you got baptized before you fully committed your life to Jesus Christ and understood what you were doing, then you weren't baptized; you just got wet.

You Can Talk the Talk, Now Walk the Walk

Evangelism is not just an event; it is a lifestyle. "Philip was found at Azotus: and passing through he preached in all the cities, till he came to Caesarea" (Acts 8:40 KJV). Every time you encounter Philip in the New Testament, he is preaching, witnessing, or evangelizing in some way. Sharing the message of Christ was simply a lifestyle for him.

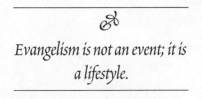

Evangelism is not an event; it is a lifestyle.

Allow the Holy Spirit to develop you into a lifestyle evangelist. Witnessing is not something forced or unnatural for you. Evangelism is something you do almost like second nature. You just talk about what Jesus has done for you all the time. The best kind of evangelism is not event evangelism, but lifestyle evangelism. The most effective evangelism is not the evangelism you do out of the church one night a week. It is the evangelism you do every day in the places where you live and work. The Great Commission literally states, "As you are going, make disciples of all nations." Wherever you go in life, make disciples of other people. Make it your lifestyle.

Make it your life.

Part Seven:

The Servant Leader

Chapter 24

A Servant Leader
Named John

〜〜〜

America suffers from a major leadership vacuum. Standards of America's citizens have fallen so low that being a smooth talker able to orchestrate a slick, top-quality presentation is more important than possessing moral fortitude and exemplary ethics. We've not only accepted moral deficiencies and failure of good judgment from leadership over the past thirty years; we've come to expect them. We've collectively stated, inasmuch as our majority vote speaks, that we willingly support and follow leaders who govern not by principle but by polls of popular opinion. The leadership vacuum resulting from their elections has swept through the nation, beyond government, into our churches and homes. From the White House to the church house to the family house, Americans critically need, but they are not receiving, genuine leadership.

If you doubt a dangerous leadership vacuum exists in America today, consider our society's condition. Look at our schools, churches, and homes. Leadership is absent in all of them. Too often, Americans vote for and follow the "pied piping" of leaders elevated to the position simply because they were considered the lesser of two evils. Too often, Americans listen to and follow preaching of church leaders who are ashamed of the gospel of Jesus Christ, who are more concerned with being politically correct than being scripturally accurate. Too often, American children commute between the homes of divorced parents or never receive the parenting of the man they long to call daddy. Every time a leader is selected based on a lesser degree of evil, cracks in our homes, churches, and country spread more dangerously across our landscape. The only question left to answer is how soon our nation will completely crumble.

Everything—everything—rises and falls on leadership.

Nature abhors a vacuum. Nature's answer to any level of leadership vacuum is an immediate, chaotic, anarchistic implosion. All human structures, institutions, and societies implode in a leadership vacuum. To live amidst such a widespread, all-encompassing leadership vacuum at every level of society places you in a dangerous situation.

This issue has everything to do with you. Every person has a leadership role at some level. Author John Maxwell simply defined *leadership* as influence.[9] Every person exerts influence upon somebody else. Government leaders influence society. Business leaders influence employees. Pastors influence congregations. Sunday school teachers influence their pupils. Husbands influence wives and children. Wives and mothers influence children. Senior-high students influence junior-high students. Influence, to some degree, is unavoidable. Every person reading this book (but don't look over your shoulder, this is for you) is responsible for some kind of leadership role in life. Maxwell pointed out, "Sociologists tell us that even the most introverted individual will influence ten thousand people during his or her lifetime!"[10] You have some areas of life in which you are being led. In other areas, you lead. The question is not whether you will lead, but instead, "What kind of leader you will be?"

History is full of leaders. Adolph Hitler, Joseph Stalin, Mao Tse Tung, Joseph Smith, and Jim Jones were all leaders. Louis Farrakahn and Saddam Hussein are leaders today. The world does not need any more of this type of leader. Jesus condemned authoritarian, egotistical, dictatorial leaders as being part of this fallen world system. Today's world does not just need leaders; it needs servant leaders. This world needs the leadership style of the person named Jesus. America doesn't just need any kind of leader; America needs "Jesus' kind of leaders." We need servant leaders:

> *America doesn't just need any kind of leader; America needs "Jesus' kind of leaders."*

Jesus called them together and said, "You know that the rulers of the Gentiles lord it over them, and their high officials exercise authority over them. Not so with you. Instead, whoever wants to become great among you must be your servant, and whoever wants to be first must be your slave (Matt. 20:25–27).

You will find one particular person in the Bible who was the kind of servant leader Jesus Christ wants you to be. Jesus himself said this person was the "greatest man who was ever born." He is the last of the Old Testament-type of prophets. His name is John the Baptist, and his life's example demonstrates how a real servant leader leads:

After this, Jesus and his disciples went out into the Judean countryside, where he spent some time with them, and baptized. Now John also was baptizing at Aenon near Salim, because there was plenty of water, and people were constantly coming to be baptized. (This was before John was put in prison.) An argument developed between some of John's disciples and a certain Jew over the matter of ceremonial washing. They came to John and said to him, "Rabbi, that man who was with you on the other side of the Jordan—the one you testified about—well, he is baptizing, and everyone is going to him."

To this John replied, "A man can receive only what is given him from heaven. You yourselves can testify that I said, 'I am not the Christ but am sent ahead of him.' The bride belongs to the bridegroom. The friend who attends the bridegroom waits and listens for him, and is full of joy when he hears the bridegroom's voice. That joy is mine, and it is now complete. He must become greater; I must become less" (John 3:22–30).

The King James Version simply says, "He must increase, but I must decrease" (v. 30). All who know Christ should want him to increase. The only way he can increase is for you to decrease.

John's servant spirit was transparent. He knew no jealousy, even when word spread that Jesus and his disciples were baptizing more people and drawing larger crowds than he was. John felt no threat of territoriality. He possessed no bitterness or hostility. John rejoiced that Jesus had begun his public ministry. John rejoiced that he could point people to Jesus. John was a great leader, but he knew that he must decrease and Jesus must increase.

John the Baptist was a strong, dynamic leader of people. Crowds flocked to him through his ministry. If a leader is someone with influence and followers, John the Baptist fit the bill. He quickly rose to prominence; his fame spread throughout the country. The people who followed him considered him a prophet from God:

In those days John the Baptist came, preaching in the Desert of Judea and saying, "Repent, for the kingdom of heaven is near." This is he who was spoken of through the prophet Isaiah:

"A voice of one calling in the desert,
'Prepare the way for the Lord,
    make straight paths for him.'"

John's clothes were made of camel's hair, and he had a leather belt around his waist. His food was locusts and wild honey. People went out to him from Jerusalem and all Judea and the whole region of the Jordan. Confessing their sins, they were baptized by him in the Jordan river (Matt. 3:1–6).

John the Baptist also had many disciples who followed him. Wherever you locate John in the Bible, you see a contingent of his disciples following and working with and for him. Andrew, the brother of Peter, was one of those disciples:

> The next day John was there again with two of his disciples. When he saw Jesus passing by, he said, "Look, the Lamb of God!"
>
> When the two disciples heard him say this, they followed Jesus. Turning around Jesus saw them following and asked, "What do you want?"
>
> They said, "Rabbi," (which means Teacher), "where are you staying?"
>
> "Come," he replied, "and you will see."
>
> So they went and saw where he was staying, and spent that day with him. It was about the tenth hour.
>
> Andrew, Simon Peter's brother, was one of the two who heard what John had said and who had followed Jesus. The first thing Andrew did was to find his brother Simon and tell him, "We have found the Messiah" (that is, the Christ). Then he brought him to Jesus (John 1:35–42).

Religious leaders feared John the Baptist. He was absolutely relentless in his condemnation of the hypocrisy of the religious establishment and its leaders in his day:

But when he saw many of the Pharisees and Sadducees coming to where he was baptizing, he said to them: "You brood of vipers! Who warned you to flee from the coming wrath? Produce fruit in keeping with repentance. And do not think you can say to yourselves, 'We have Abraham as our father,' I tell you that out of these stones God can raise up children for Abraham. The ax is already at the root of the trees, and every tree that does not produce good fruit will be cut down and thrown into the fire" (Matt. 3:7–10).

Religious leaders did not like John the Baptist because every time he had an opportunity he blasted them. They could not touch him because he was so popular and powerful. Even Herod, the cruel Roman puppet king, was fascinated by John the Baptist:

They went out and preached that people should repent. They drove out many demons and anointed many sick people with oil and healed them.

King Herod heard about this, for Jesus' name had become well known. Some were saying, "John the Baptist has been raised from the dead, and that is why miraculous powers are at work in him."

Others said, "He is Elijah."

And still others claimed, "He is a prophet, like one of the prophets of long ago."

But when Herod heard this, he said, "John, the man I beheaded, has been raised from the dead!"

For Herod himself had given orders to have John arrested, and he had him bound and put in prison. He did this because of Herodias, his brother Philip's wife, whom he had married.

> For John had been saying to Herod, "It is not lawful for you to have your brother's wife." So Herodias nursed a grudge against John and wanted to kill him. But she was not able to, because Herod feared John and protected him, knowing him to be a righteous and holy man. When Herod heard John, he was greatly puzzled; yet he liked to listen to him (Mark 6:12–20).

Jesus provided the greatest confirmation of John the Baptist's leadership, stating, "I tell you the truth: Among those born of women there has not risen anyone greater than John the Baptist; yet he who is least in the kingdom of heaven is greater than he" (Matt. 11:11).

John the Baptist was a powerful, influential man and one of the greatest leaders who ever lived. More important than his greatness was his leadership style. He was not only a leader; he was the right kind of leader. He was a servant leader. You, too, are a leader. Are you a servant leader? The popular, fearless, baptizing prophet John said the same words that should fall from your lips with each leadership opportunity: "He must increase. I must decrease."

Chapter 25

Calling All Leaders

∽∽∽

Every autumn, high school boys gather on expansive fields and battle as grown men. At the same time, grown men—before crowds of thousands—play the game of high school boys. Americans love football, both as spectators and competitors. The sport certainly has superstars, players who can throw four touchdowns or rush one hundred yards nearly every game or defenders whose skills change opponents' game plans. Football is undeniably a team sport.

Each August, when coaches scout athletes competing on the gridiron for a roster spot, they know their task is to assemble the best team possible. They gather players to evaluate agility, speed, size, strength, quickness, and overall ability. Each player will be assigned to a certain position according to skill and physical makeup, with the expectation that he will help the team be as balanced as possible. Coaches know that no championship team on any level ever consisted solely of linemen. Though they are the biggest men on the field, they are strategically used to protect the quarterback and block for the running back, rather than to score touchdowns themselves. They cannot throw, run, or kick as well as the men behind them. The coach looks for the persons most appropriate to fit the needed positions, and he fills his roster accordingly.

Even coaches recognize that a player's God-given equipment is what makes each competitor successful. Natural abilities and body type are not taught elements of the game. God bestows these on people. Having a huge desire is helpful, but it isn't always enough. That's why the National Football League doesn't have five-foot-five, 165-pound linemen blocking for John Elway, Dan Marino, Barry Sanders, or Terrell Davis. Coaches make their living finding the right man for the job, knowing exactly what it takes to fill each position.

God is the ultimate coach. His game is life, and he coaches it more seriously and with greater strategy than any coach coaches the Super Bowl. God knows what gifts are best suited for his roster. As genetics predispose a football player to a certain position, God gives each of us certain skills that assign us to a specific job.

John the Baptist is a perfect example. Before he was even born, God called him to be the front-runner to the Christ. He was chosen by God to be a prophet and forerunner of the Messiah, miraculously announced at his birth by the angel to his father, Zechariah:

> In the time of Herod king of Judea there was a priest named Zechariah, who belonged to the priestly division of Abijah; his wife Elizabeth was also a descendant of Aaron. Both of them were upright in the sight of God, observing all the Lord's commandments and regulations blamelessly. But they had no children, because Elizabeth was barren; and they were both well along in years.

> Once when Zechariah's division was on duty and he was serving as priest before God, he was chosen by lot, according to the custom of the priesthood, to go into the temple of the Lord and burn incense. And when the time for the burning of incense came, all the assembled worshipers were praying outside.

Then an angel of the Lord appeared to him, standing at the right side of the altar of incense. When Zechariah saw him, he was startled and was gripped with fear. But the angel said to him: "Do not be afraid, Zechariah; your prayer has been heard. Your wife Elizabeth will bear you a son, and you are to give him the name John. He will be a joy and delight to you, and many will rejoice because of his birth, for he will be great in the sight of the Lord. He is never to take wine or other fermented drink, and he will be filled with the Holy Spirit even from birth. Many of the people of Israel will he bring back to the Lord their God. And he will go on before the Lord, in the spirit and power of Elijah, to turn the hearts of the fathers to their children and the disobedient to the wisdom of the righteous—to make ready a people prepared for the Lord" (Luke 1:5–17).

Before John was born, even before he was conceived in his mother's womb, God had a special and specific plan for him. John lived his life with a sense of call. God also has a special plan and purpose for your life. You too can live your life with a sense of call and mission, knowing you have been chosen by God. "You did not choose me, but I chose you to go and bear fruit—fruit that will last. Then the Father will give you whatever you ask in my name" (John 15:16).

Living on Purpose

When your life has a sense of call, you live purposefully. John knew his exact purpose:

* "He himself was not the light; he came only as a witness to the light—" (John 1:8).
* He was not the Christ but was sent ahead of him (John 3:27–28).
* He was not the bridegroom but an attendant to the bridegroom (John 3:29).

John knew his purpose, exactly what he was to do. His clear sense of purpose allowed him to lead influentially. Do you have a clear sense of purpose and mission in your life today? Do you know exactly how God equipped you and what he called you to do? Do you know what you are supposed to be doing with your life right now?

Do you have a clear sense of purpose and mission in your life today?

If you don't know the purpose for which God has called you, it is impossible to know whether you are doing it. Simply to slide through life with no sense of purpose or direction would be both sadly fatalistic and perpetually fruitless. To "let life happen" to you makes you reactionary, never taking actions to move continually forward with God's plans for you. Without a strong sense of divine purpose in life, you will never be a leader. Nobody wants to follow someone who has no idea where to go or why to go there.

Coloring Life Within the Lines

Living with a sense of call gives you clear parameters. John knew his parameters because he knew his life's specific divine call, and it helped him live within the confines of what God created him to do. It also kept him from being jealous or envious of people who had a different purpose or mission. Since John knew he was not the light, he was not jealous of the light, nor did he try to be the light. Since John knew he was not the Christ, he was not jealous of the one who was the Christ, nor did he try to be the Christ. Since John knew he was not the bridegroom, he was not jealous of the one who received the bride, nor did he attempt to take the bride.

You get in trouble when you try to be someone you were not called or equipped to be. Don't be jealous of someone with different parameters than yours. Don't try to be someone you weren't designed to be. Don't feel guilty when someone asks you to do something outside your parameters. You can say no because you know that is not what God desires for your life:

For by the grace given me I say to every one of you: Do not think of yourself more highly than you ought, but rather think of yourself with sober judgment, in accordance with the measure of faith God has given you. Just as each of us has one body with many members, and these members do not all have the same function, so in Christ we who are many form one body, and each member belongs to all the others (Rom. 12:3–5).

Living the Passionate Life

Living with a sense of call gives you passion. John the Baptist approached his mission and calling in life with fervency and passion. He was driven. Nobody had to jump-start John. He was an initiator whose call consumed him. His passion was so obvious in his preaching and ministry; it drew masses to him and made him extremely effective. From the day this long-haired, unshaven prophet, wearing a camel-hair coat and eating wild locusts and honey, came thundering from the desert, he preached a fiery, zealous message of repentance. Passion drove the voice of one crying in the wilderness (Isa. 40:3). There was nothing dull about this passionate guy.

A great weakness in today's leaders is a lack of passion. Many are indifferently lazy. They have to be jump-started. Some lack vision or initiative. Many are totally oblivious to what needs to be done as the world collapses around them. They stand dazed, not knowing what to do, waiting to be told, or waiting for someone else to do it. They have no passion; some are really boring. This lack of passion is an incalculable void in church leadership. Effective leaders must be consumed by and passionate about their calling. When people respond to their call with the same passion God has in making the call, ministry busts out all over!

Passionate leaders are like racehorses pushing against the starting gate, ready to start racing. These horses run with the one purpose for which they were trained. Passionate leaders see what needs to be done, and they do it. They do not wait for assignments and directions. They initiate. They don't need supervision and are not drawn into constant accountability. They burn with the consuming, passionate fire of Christ's call. And they stay on fire, looking for more ways to fulfill their God-designed destiny. Their joys come when they are elbow-deep in passionate labor, and they sorrow when they stray from their call to fulfill other obligations.

Our church staff knows that I as pastor expect only four things:

1. Inspiration. Stay in tune with God. Keep your heart right.

2. Innovation. Be creative. Look for what needs to be done. Don't get in a rut.

3. Initiative. Be a self-starter. Don't wait to be told to do it.

4. Information. Keep me informed. I don't like surprises.

All church staff members should be as passionate about their ministry and responsibilities as John was. The church also needs more lay leaders with initiative, people who have a sense of call and passion about ministry. They drive their ministry and don't need staff management. The church needs more initiators who can see what needs to be done and do it.

God has assigned you a spot on his roster. He wants you to be a team leader. He has given you your lifetime to discover your talents and how to use them for his glory. Is your church lacking a ministry you could lead? If you know sign language, begin a deaf ministry. If you can teach, begin a tutoring ministry. If you write well, initiate a correspondence ministry. If your passion is discipleship, disciple someone. If your heart breaks for the salvation of strangers, lead visitation teams. If God placed a call on you to pastor or be a missionary, quit pretending you don't hear him. Be a person who makes church more than just a building.

Step out in obedience onto the playing field. Put on your helmet, throw on your pads. Line up in the position where God called you to be. Be a light in our world's vast darkness, a believer who is called to win the lost for their eternal championship victory in Christ.

Chapter 26

The Character Issue

❦❦❦

The bright studio lighting would have cooked the two candidates if it weren't for the perspiration absorbing the makeup caked on their faces. They were about to enter a debate vital to the election. Both must be witty, dynamic, convincing. Both must attack without bared teeth yet bite deeply enough that his foe could not recover from the wounds. The incumbent prepared a salvo of missiles directed toward his challenger's shady business dealings and questionable ethics. The young politico with more aspirations than experience had an array of third- and fourth-hand accounts of the incumbent's notorious, extramarital philandering.

No sooner were the introductions tendered than the challenger made a decision. His best offense fired every cannon at once, hoping to defeat the enemy before the voters' attention span drove them to change channels to a rerun of "America's Funniest Videos." He leaned into the microphone and sharply gave the "fire" command by asking, "Since you came into office, much evidence has come to light that you have had numerous liaisons outside the sanctity of your marriage relationship. How do you, first of all, respond to the charges; and how do you plan to be an effective leader, with this hanging over your head for the entirety of the term, should our constituency make the grave error of reelecting you?"

The incumbent looked briefly at a sheet on his podium with a prepared answer to such a question. The only surprise was that the question came so early. The incumbent, though, saw his opportunity. If delivered correctly, his reply would turn all the challenger's weapons around and quite possibly cause his opponent to succumb to a terminal shot in the foot.

He leaned forward and calmly stated through smiling teeth: "I will not make character an issue of this campaign. I stand by my record on policy issues. If you feel you must resort to character attacks to win this election, I am confident the voters will recognize your tactics."

In this day and age, such tactics work. Leaders somehow separate character from performance. One word explains the idea that character is not important to leadership—*stupid*. Character can no more be separated from leadership than bitterness from lemons. They simply go together.

Servant leaders are identified by character. They earn the right to lead by the virtue of their character. Those with no character have no right to lead. Job applications almost always ask the question, "Have you ever been arrested?" Those who answer yes have to answer the follow-up question, "Why?" The world of employment leadership realizes that character and leadership are indivisible.

~

Integrity: Do the Right Thing

John the Baptist was a dynamic leader because he was a person of character. His character is seen in his integrity, made visible in his personal holiness. Even Herod knew John the Baptist to be a righteous man (Mark 6:20). Personal holiness was important to him. His life was above reproach. No scandals swirled around him or his ministry.

Other people see your integrity if it is indeed present. Integrity keeps you from compromising your morals and belief systems. Integrity allows you to stand firm when you are persecuted for your faith. Integrity keeps you from viewing movies, watching TV shows, reading books, or scanning magazines that debase you and do nothing to edify humanity. Integrity propels you to persevere when the world sees only failure. Integrity compels you to continue speaking a message even when the world hears and labels you a fool because of it.

~

Honesty Is Such a Lonely Word

John the Baptist's character is seen in his personal honesty. With John, what you see is what you get. John was the same, no matter who was in his company. He spoke the truth even when speaking to a king, knowing full well it could cost him his head. Nobody ever got double-talk from John. John had little concern with being "politically correct." He was far more concerned about simply being correct.

Our day is filled with double-talk and promise-breaking. You may know people who don't admit mistakes. They make excuses or blame someone else or even lie. They will never say: "I am fully responsible for what happened. I blew it!" If you want to lead effectively, be a person of deep integrity, of personal holiness and honesty. Be genuine, not hypocritical. Mean what you say, and say what you mean. Keep promises. Let your word be your bond.

~

To God Be the Glory

John's character is seen in his humility. Even though he was a folk hero and a popular preacher/prophet, fame or success never went to his head. He remained greatly humble. When Jesus arrived, John pointed others to him. John lifted up Jesus in every action and statement:

> "I baptize you with water for repentance. But after me will come one who is more powerful than I, whose sandals I am not fit to carry. He will baptize you with the Holy Spirit and with fire. His winnowing fork is in his hand, and he will clear his threshing floor, gathering his wheat into the barn and burning up the chaff with unquenchable fire."

> Then Jesus came from Galilee to the Jordan to be baptized by John. But John tried to deter him, saying, "I need to be baptized by you, and do you come to me?"
>
> Jesus replied, "Let it be so now; it is proper for us to do this to fulfill all righteousness." Then John consented (Matt. 3:11–15).

Servant leaders aren't boastful, proud, aloof, arrogant, combative, or egotistical. A humble leader does not lead by dictatorial demands but by example. They are gentle and respectful to the people who follow.

~

Selfish Is Not a Seafood Delicacy

John's character is seen in his unselfishness. He had to be one of the most unselfish humans who ever lived. When Jesus began his ministry, many of the people who had been following John the Baptist began to follow Jesus. Even some of John's closest disciples and associates left him to join ranks with Jesus. One of the two disciples who left John to follow Jesus was Andrew, the brother of Simon Peter (John 1:35–42). These brothers eventually became two of Christ's twelve apostles. Peter could have easily become a disciple of John the Baptist instead of Jesus had John been selfish or territorial in regard to his ministry.

A true servant leader is unselfish. Protectionism and territorialism do not exist. A servant leader is concerned with God's Kingdom, not individual earthly kingdoms. When a minister starts a new church, the greatest resistance often does not come from unbelievers or from churches of other denominations. Primary opposition comes from churches of the same denomination. Some pastors and churches fear that new congregations will encroach upon their "territory." When reaching people, don't be selfish. Churches should make room for evangelism, discipleship, and education, not selfishness or territorialism.

Servant leaders are needed in Sunday schools. Churches need teachers and directors who are totally unselfish, who are not the least bit territorial or self-protective. Teachers can't be territorial about their room or their class. Churches need leaders with servants' hearts who just want to help wherever they can be used, who are available to do whatever needs to be done, and who serve wherever they can make a contribution. Churches need these people for leaders.

～

Psst . . . Your Leadership Is Showing

John's character is seen in his transparency. He was confident and courageous. Yet he was not without some weaknesses. He was even given to moments of discouragement and doubt. When he was imprisoned for challenging Herod, concerning the king's adultery with his brother's wife, John became discouraged. It is unclear how long he was in prison before Herod actually was tricked into beheading him, but it was an extended time. While imprisoned, John received reports of Jesus' work and ministry. Honestly, Jesus was not acting how John had assumed the Messiah would, and Jesus was not doing what John expected him to do. And even though John the Baptist had seen an eyewitness confirmation when the dove descended upon Jesus at baptism, he began to doubt. Perhaps the doubt came from the discouragement and emotional strain of being locked in a dungeon, or perhaps John's unfulfilled expectations of Jesus led him to question if Jesus was truly the Messiah. Regardless, John was honestly transparent about his questions. He did the right thing when he doubted; he went straight to Jesus:

> After Jesus had finished instructing his twelve disciples, he went on from there to teach and preach in the towns of Galilee.

> When John heard in prison what Christ was doing, he sent his disciples to ask him, "Are you the one who was to come, or should we expect someone else?"

> Jesus replied, "Go back and report to John what you hear and see: The blind receive sight, the lame walk, those who have leprosy are cured, the deaf hear, the dead are raised, and the good news is preached to the poor. Blessed is the man who does not fall away on account of me" (Matt. 11:1–6).

John was a great, courageous, confident leader; yet he still had moments of discouragement and doubt. He was transparent and did not try to hide it. Your strength shows when you admit weaknesses and struggles and when you are honest about moments of doubt and discouragement.

Servant leaders do not maintain a false, impregnable mask of perfection. Those whom you serve and lead appreciate when you honestly and openly share weaknesses and discouragement. They will know you are genuine. Everyone experiences discouraging moments of doubt. We all have cracked dams restraining our questions and insecurities. Don't try to maintain images of perfection and strength. When you hurt or doubt, be transparent. Each day you face character issues. Often, character will be the only issue. Maintain integrity. Be honest, humble, and unselfish. Let your humanity be transparent. Lead with character.

Chapter 27

Be Strong and
Take Courage

~~~

"I dare you," Sam, age ten, said to his younger brother.

"How high up are we?" Zach asked.

"Eight feet," Sam answered calmly.

That's one foot for every year of my life, Zach thought. He looked down nervously and gulped in fear. "I double-dare you," he replied with a momentary thought of superiority.

Sam peered from atop the shed's roof where they stood, wearing identical purple capes that their grandmother had given them last Christmas. They had enjoyed secret identities as Batman and Robin for months. With summer announcing its arrival with a dry, sunny day, their mother sent the caped crusaders outside to continue their escapades. In the course of chasing imaginary villains, the brothers climbed the stack of logs behind the shed and mounted the roof. The eight-foot-tall structure suddenly became the Empire State Building. The only way down for a superhero was to jump. The only question: Which superhero would be the first to take the plunge and sprain an ankle or even something worse?

Sam thought he knew the unfortunate answer as he inched toward the roof's tiled edge. Eight feet looked like eighty feet. Then, with a revelation that comes only when having two more years of life gives you a 20 percent advantage in experience, Sam turned and, barely audibly, whispered, "I double-dog dare you."

This time, Zach's gulp stuck in his throat like a toothpick swallowed sideways. The ultimatum had been extended. This volley of challenges would go no further. Zach knew what this meant. He had no choice. He stepped to the edge with as much confidence as an eight-year-old can muster. He slowly crouched to minimize the distance from his eyes to the turf below. He took one final look over his shoulder to Sam, still grinning smugly at his small victory. The moment had arrived; Zach could wait no longer. He slowly filled his lungs with breezy warm air. He summoned every bit of courage possible, tapping into reserves he didn't know existed before that moment. He paused one last second for drama, and, as powerfully as possible . . . he yelled. "MOMMMMY! HELP ME!"

Zach one day will become a great leader. He found enough courage to analyze a situation and take the safe option. He took the long look and decided it was smarter to swallow his pride and get down safely. It took more courage to overcome an older brother's inevitable teasing and ensure he could chase villains another day than it did to leap from the shed to whatever injury awaited. Rather than look brave and jump to doom, Zach was brave, yelling until his mother rescued them (and later lectured them about climbing on rooftops).

Servant leaders are always identified by the courage they demonstrate in leadership. Often, you will face the same decision as Zach. You will have to choose between looking like you have courage and taking a leap or showing you have the courage to make a smart decision and lead others to safety. Your courage will reveal whether you are a servant leader.

~

Courage to Share

John the Baptist had the courage to share his accomplishments and applause. He had a well-established ministry, and his fame was spreading by the time Jesus arrived. Some thought Jesus was a Johnny-come-lately who was encroaching on John's territory and taking his spotlight. John simply responded to their complaints: "He must increase, but I must decrease" (John 3:30 KJV).

Leonard Bernstein once reportedly said, "The most difficult position to fill in an orchestra is second fiddle." It takes courage to be willing to play second fiddle. Servant leaders have the courage to step out of the spotlight and share victories and accolades of successes with others. True servant leaders intentionally do not promote themselves or boast of themselves. They intentionally move attention to others. They intentionally decrease so others can increase.

The church needs to learn this today. There is so much self-exaltation among contemporary leaders of the church. Churches today work so hard to have slick-finished brochures and marketing campaigns and publicity strategies. They work so hard to promote their greatness and to bring in new members that bragging about accomplishments seems normal. However, the bragging becomes so boastful that many church leaders are actually beginning to believe their own press reports about themselves. A true leader is courageous enough to share the accomplishments and applause.

Don't forget that you never go into ministry alone. If you do, you are doing it wrong. If you are doing ministry correctly, the Lord Jesus is constantly accompanying you. As such, Jesus should receive all your praise. If you venture into ministry with other people, don't forget to send some praise and accolade in their direction. While the ultimate desire behind ministry should simply be ministry, people like to be recognized for their efforts. Don't take complete credit for success when you have a staff of volunteers who do the legwork and the Holy Spirit who does the heart work. Share the praise with others and give the praise to God.

The Truth, the Whole Truth, and Nothing but the Truth

John had the courage to speak the truth. People never had to wonder where they stood on any subject

> *Your responsibility is always to speak the truth in love.*

with John the Baptist because he was brutally honest. He always had the courage to speak the truth about Jesus. He spoke the truth about the Pharisees and the teachers of the law of his day. He even spoke the truth to Herod, not intimidated by even a king. You have to appreciate someone who has the courage to be honest and speak the truth at all times.

Stand Up for What You Believe In

John courageously stood by his convictions. John told King Herod he was wrong for living in adultery with his brother's wife, Herodias. John stood by his convictions, even when they were not "politically correct" and when it was bad for his health. Standing by his convictions eventually cost John his head. A servant leader has the courage to speak out when others shrink like wilting flowers in late day heat. To be humble and meek does not mean to be wishy-washy and weak; "A double minded man is unstable in all his ways" (James 1:8 KJV).

A servant does not try to capitulate or cater to every person. Servants stand by convictions and inspire others to follow. The early Christian martyrs were so brave in their convictions that they died terrible, horrible deaths for their faith in God. The aim of martyring

> *To be humble and meek does not mean to be wishy-washy and weak.*

Christians was to quell the Christian movement. It failed, and Christianity exploded. Many people saw that the martyrs' God was real and different. They inspired countless others to follow God. Contemporary martyrs continue to inspire people to faith today because their courage to stand by convictions in Christ is a life-and-death testimony unmatched by preaching.

Find the source of your courage, then tap that source daily. Be strong and take courage.

Chapter 28

The Long and Winding Road

∽∾∽∾

Every time you enter into a covenant or make a commitment, you put yourself at risk. Any covenant relationship you enter into will, over the course of its term, reveal the measure to which you can be held accountable for your commitment promise. By honoring the covenant, you demonstrate to others that your word is your bond. By breaking the commitment, you show that your word is not as strong as the adversity that challenges the covenant.

In life, you often enter into commitments. Those commitments carry different restrictions and limitations and are structured for various time limits. Many will require much from you; some are thankfully easy to honor. Commitments are everywhere. When you sign an employment contract, you are signing a commitment that you will agree to work for a predetermined period of time, for a predetermined salary. If you don't adequately perform the tasks outlined in the written commitment, you can legally be terminated from the position.

Many people treat credit cards as instant cash. They believe that the more cards they carry, the more purchase power they have. The truth is, the credit card is little more than a mobile, transferable covenant binder. Every time a clerk swipes your card through the register to pay a bill, the card registers another commitment to your debt load. Every purchase is a covenant that you will pay as quickly as possible. Failure to complete full payment results in added annual interest up to as much as 21 percent of the remaining balance.

Too often, people can look at all the covenants they have entered and feel overwhelmed, unable to handle all the responsibilities to which they willingly agreed. The search for relief and escape begins. This search has brought about such popular terms as "no-fault divorce" and "declaring bankruptcy." Throughout modern history, we have created loopholes, where none existed before, in order to jump out the back window of covenant relationships.

~

Be Prepared

John the Baptist was completely committed to the ministry God had given him. John's commitment is shown in his preparation. He gave his entire life in preparation for a very brief ministry, "And the child grew and became strong in spirit; and he lived in the desert until he appeared publicly to Israel" (Luke 1:80). God placed John in the home of godly parents, Elizabeth and the priest Zechariah, so they might protect and train him for the specific mission God had for him. They were given special instruction on how to raise John: "He is never to take wine or other fermented drink, and he will be filled with the Holy Spirit even from birth" (Luke 1:15).

If you are called to be a leader, demonstrate your commitment to that call by paying the price in preparation. If you are called to preach, you are called to prepare. Go to school; get all the education you can. While formal education does not make the preacher—only the Holy Spirit of God can do that—he who takes his call seriously pays whatever price necessary to prepare and train. When a man is willing to go through four years of college and at least three years of seminary, knowing he may get out and take a church that cannot even pay him a living wage, that demonstrates the discipline and commitment necessary to be an effective leader.

The same is true for other ministry: If you are going to teach the Bible or lead a ministry, pay the price in preparation. Apply this to any ministry, any leadership imaginable. The key to effective leadership is in total commitment and paying the price in preparation.

Committed to the Gospel

John's commitment was also evidenced in his preaching. "In those days John the Baptist came, preaching in the Desert of Judea and saying, 'Repent, for the kingdom of heaven is near'" (Matt. 3:1–2). The message of repentance has never been popular. People don't like being told they are wrong or they have sinned and stand condemned before God. Nobody wants to be told to repent. We'd rather hear a soft sermon on "Five Easy Steps to Feeling Good about Yourself." The message of repentance is still not popular today, so few preachers preach it. Preaching repentance keeps a preacher from appearing seeker-sensitive.

John preached the message of repentance even when it was not popular and when he was criticized for preaching it. The Pharisees and the Sadducees didn't come to participate in John's crusade or support his ministry. They came to poke fun, criticize, and taunt this country preacher. His response to their critical cynicism was simple and loving. He kept on preaching the message he was told to preach: Repent! He even turned up the heat a little for the Pharisees and the Sadducees.

Evangelism should be a firm root of all ministry. Christ's love should perpetually shine through. A message of repentance should always be shared. Every time God's word is silenced due to "political correctness," the adversary claims a victory.

~

Taking One for the Team

John's commitment is shown in his persecution. He stayed faithful to his mission and his message even when it cost him imprisonment and eventually execution. Certainly John knew his message was dangerous. Telling the king he is living in sin always brings stiff retribution. John was committed to God, his word, and his truth. As long as he honored his commitments, he was willing to let the result take care of itself.

The commitment Jesus Christ gave to you was for eternity. He forgave you before you ever first sinned. He never turned his back on you. He turned his back toward the whips of Roman soldiers in place of you. His commitment sticks. He is committed to using you to bring in other believers. He is committed to loving you and using you, regardless of how poorly you keep your commitment to him. A servant leader recognizes Christ's commitment and tries to emulate it every day and in every way.

Part Eight:

The Servant and the New World Order

~~~

Chapter 29

The New World Order

～～～

We live in the age of the New World Order. Globally, governments and their economists, strategists, and politicians seem to be enamored and fascinated by the approaching New World Order, embracing unified structure and organization. However, the nebulous term *New World Order* has as many definitions as there are people devoting their lives to its organization. To some the term means "a unified global government." To others it means a global military defense system. For some, it means a single global economic system, propelled by a single monetary system eliminating exchange inadequacies and improving international commerce. For still others, the New World Order is an amalgam of some or all of those components. The phrase has come to refer to an impending global transition. The world is evolving this very moment toward the New World Order.

For this evolution to flourish, the New World Order relies on a worldly approach to growth as old as sin itself. The same characteristics guiding our world's current and future leaders are the same characteristics the

215

majority of leaders have demonstrated throughout history. In reality, the established New World Order will be nothing more than an extreme advance of the world's very old, very effective, deceptive ways of advancing leaders and manipulating others for the gain of power, prestige, and position. To see how the New World Order will be, view past and present leadership and allow it time to fester.

The Gaze of Narcissus

This present world system is driven by prideful self-love. Leaders today often aspire to office not for how they can serve but for the relative immortality that being elected provides. They want an office because they are in love with themselves and what they have to offer. They think the office would be in peril if anybody else filled the vacancy. The New World Order proceeds because current leaders think that unity will remove opposition obstacles from the path of peace. These people claim idealistic motives, but the driving motive is self-love.

The same self-love guided men's actions in the days of Jesus:

> Then the mother of Zebedee's sons came to Jesus with her sons and, kneeling down, asked a favor of him.
>
> "What is it you want?" he asked.
>
> She said, "Grant that one of these two sons of mine may sit at your right and the other at your left in your kingdom."
>
> "You don't know what you are asking," Jesus said to them. "Can you drink the cup I am going to drink?"
>
> "We can," they answered
>
> Jesus said to them, "You will indeed drink from my cup, but to sit at my right or left is not for me to grant. These places belong to those for whom they have been prepared by my Father" (Matt. 20:20–23).

James and John had to have been filled with pride and self-love to be able to make the request they made of Jesus. Their request was verbalized by their mother Salome.

Salome is much like one of today's outspoken Little League baseball moms. This type of mom storms the field, dragging her little, skinny, cross-eyed, knock-kneed kid by the arm. She confronts the poor guy volunteering to coach the scraggly, talent-deficient team. She proudly puts her face inches from his and yells how her kid is a pitching prodigy and why her kid ought to start. Her kid doesn't even know on which hand to wear the glove but feels like the hottest prospect since Babe Ruth because mother keeps saying so. Reluctantly, the coach relents. The coach hands the child the ball. Mom trots off victoriously. Her kid mounts the pitcher's mound, winds up, and chucks the ball over the backstop and into the stands.

Jesus was just like that coach. He volunteered to lead a world full of talent-deficient team members and selected a starting squad of disciples who had as many flaws as features. He faced the same situation as that coach when Salome confronted him. Jesus responded like the coach, once he heard Salome's request. He looked at James and John and asked, "Can you boys drink of the cup I am about to drink?" James and John don't even hesitate. "We can, Coach. Put us in the game!"

Pride and self-love controlled the hearts of James and John. They evaluated what they assumed would happen when Jesus established his kingdom and essentially said: "Jesus, we want to be ahead of Adam. We want to be over Abraham, Isaac, and Jacob and to supervise Moses. We can manage Daniel, Isaiah, and Jeremiah. We thought about it, and we're obviously the preferred choice among your disciples. Our aptitudes and abilities are ahead of the pack." These two would never be accused of being shy. They certainly were not suffering from a lack of self-esteem. No wonder Jesus nicknamed them "the Sons of Thunder" (Mark 3:17).

James and John were caught up in the sinful pride of a fallen world system driven by a flawed, cultic perception of self. "Selfism" is an encompassing sin that includes the practices of self-love, self-actualization, self-promotion, self-esteem, and self-exaltation. The system has no room for God, Jesus Christ, or the Holy Spirit. Satan was a member of that cult system of self. He became filled with self-pride and wanted a high position. He wanted to displace God and rule the universe. When he failed, he wanted to infect the human race with the same sinful, self-centered pride that poisoned him. He tempted our ancient parents, Adam and Eve, with the lie: "God is holding out on you. Eat this and you will become like God."

Sadly, Adam and Eve believed him. Consequently, today's culture is absolutely drunk on the pride of self-love. Satan told us we deserved better, and we believed him. Our misplaced trust in that lie is why it is so trendy to talk about self-actualization, self-esteem, self-love, self-image, and self-fulfillment. We have become full believers in the "selfism" cult. Even sadder, the church was seduced by the same lie and has bought into the same fallen thinking. Make note of how many books in your Christian bookstore are based more on trendy pop psychology than on solid biblical theology. Many books are feeding the carnal flesh of humanity with themes of self-esteem and self-love. Unfortunately, psychobabble is directing the actions of Christian laypeople and church leaders. In it all, the gospel of Jesus Christ is lost.

~

If You Scratch My Back . . .

Political self-promotion characterizes the New World Order. People gain power through the people they know and to whom they profess allegiances. Values, ethics, and morals are trivial. Today, it is more important for people to prove loyalty by politically, professionally, and socially assassinating friends, coworkers, even family, while promoting themselves and like-minded others. Actions of deception, persuasion, coercion, and subversion guarantee promotion. Leaders on every level have developed a network allowing the advance of heartless underlings while at the same time weeding out undesirables with other interests at heart. The political nature of the current world system helps ensure the success of the incoming New World Order as well as the failure of any opposition.

James and John familiarized themselves with this political self-promotion system. The manner in which they approached Jesus was very political. They had their mother make the request for them. Salome was Jesus Christ's aunt. She was Mary's sister. Aunt Salome approached Jesus on behalf of his own first cousins. Controversial enough that Christ's own aunt approached him, the manner in which she confronted him was political. She bowed before him, an obvious tactic of manipulation. Bowing was a way of currying to Jesus' favor by showing him obedience and reverence. Furthermore, Aunt Salome framed her request by kneeling to ask him a favor. Imagine the scene: Aunt Salome walks up to Christ with her two boys, holding each by the arm like scruffy dolls. She walks up to Jesus and bows down to him. Jesus thinks, *I can't believe she's really going through with this.*

"Jesus, darling," she says, her voice dripping with sugary sweetness "You know you are my favorite nephew, don't you? Remember that toy chariot I gave you on your fifth birthday? Remember how many nights you used to stay over at our house and play with Jimmy and Johnny? Remember how I used to get up early and make your favorite cinnamon-raisin bagels for breakfast? Well, Jesus, I was just wondering if you would do your Aunt Salome just one teensy-weensy favor . . . please, just one little thing for your favorite Aunt Salome?"

Her methods may be nauseating, but you cannot deny she knew how our world operates. Hers was a political power play from the beginning. Things still work the same way. A popular tactic for getting ahead today is to use a friend's influence to one's own advantage. Using people's influence to get ahead in business, to gain political office, to secure a lucrative contract, or to climb the corporate ladder is commonplace. People daily do exactly what James and John did with Jesus. They tried to use their mother's influence to manipulate Jesus.

After their mom had done her best, they did a little schmoozing of their own. Only after she was finished did they approach him and say, "Jesus, we can drink of the same cup you drink. We can handle anything you can give us. We are yours. We are with you. Give us the word, give us the position, give us the power. We will go all the way with you!"

Jesus simply said, "You don't even know what you are asking."

You may need to see if you are perhaps guilty of a little politicking yourself. You might have a euphemism for it. You might not think it is politicking if you call it "networking." As a believer, don't use the manipulative activity of politicking to get ahead. Take the high road and genuinely love and serve people without any selfish motive in mind. Trust your future to God. The world has a network, and the followers of Christ have no place in it.

~

King of the Hill

Power and self-exaltation also help define this present world system. The goal of many leaders is to accumulate more power in order to use it for self-exaltation. "Having it all" no longer means having enough to enjoy the luxuries of life. It now seems to mean "getting everything you can get your hands on" to prosper at the expense of your competition. A power lust drives people to lose sight of the greater good and to compromise everything they hold sacred. People see the perks of power and become incredibly shortsighted. Nothing seems to matter. Ethics are negotiable. Relationships pale in comparison. Morals are meaningless. People become so intent on gaining power that they lavish upon themselves the exaltation that accompanies it. They literally abandon everything meaningful to do it.

James and John wanted that power, that self-exaltation. Jesus had thrice told James, John, and the other disciples where he was headed. He had told them he was headed for Jerusalem where he would be betrayed and eventually crucified, buried, and raised after three days. James and John wanted nothing to do with suffering, crucifixion, death, and burial. They totally missed what Jesus was trying to tell them. They did not want a cross; they wanted crowns. They did not want to be the door slave; they wanted to sit at the head table. They were hungry for power, position, and prestige.

Jesus warned them about being power hungry. He told them this was how the world operated, and they can't operate that way any longer. It has been said that God intended for us to love people and use things. Unfortunately, we do just the opposite. When power is gained, subordinate people are used to do tasks they themselves once did. Subjective people become objects used by those in power. People use their power to manipulate through adversity rather than deal with it ethically and honorably. Power hungry people cannot be told they are out of God's will; their consciences are impenetrable. The power-lusting consider all others expendable. The value of life has lost its meaning to them.

Earth continues its perpetual spin toward a New World Order revolution. The events now encompassed by the New World Order are the very world events prophesied by Scripture to happen in human history's final days prior to Christ's return. The numerous significant global movements and events defining the New World Order are preparing the way for the antichrist and the Great Tribulation. These movements include rapid acceleration toward a "one-world, transnational" government; a global economy; economic, political, and military consolidation of the European nations; rebirth of the nation of Israel; constant conflict in the Middle East; and the global expansion of Islam. This societal evolution is simply an adjustment to history to prepare for the arrival and ascension of the antichrist to world power.

While the current world system moves to its concept of the New World Order, it also continues its contemporary methods, practices, and ramifications. Daily, you will witness events showing that the will of God is the last thing on the mind of many current leaders. Always remember your Lord Jesus Christ is in control. You are responsible to be in this world but not of it. Follow the principles Christ himself set before you. Go where Christ goes. Within his will, you will see that only he can create the true New World Order.

Chapter 30

Leading the
New World Order

∽∾∽∾∽

Around two thousand years ago Jesus introduced a radically new and different New World Order. The only global plan for successful reorganization and international peace and prosperity was devised long before someone creative coined the term *New World Order*. While Christ's New World Order is not so well-known in the modern world, it will be the one to come to fruition. More than two thousand years ago, Jesus Christ foretold of his New World Order, who would lead it, and how it would operate. While Jesus walked among people, he demonstrated and offered a New World Order way of living. His way was unlike anything this world had ever seen or heard since the fall of Adam and Eve. His way of living will reign in the future.

Christ's new way of thinking and living is so contrary to the present world order's way of thinking and living that, when Jesus modeled it and taught it, it totally stunned most people. Few even understood it; most rejected it. Jesus clearly stated that if you are to follow him, your life will be radically different from the people around you. Your life will defy this present world system. You will think, act, and live in total opposition to the world's way of doing things:

> Jesus called them together and said, "You know that the rulers of the Gentiles lord it over them, and their high officials exercise authority over them. Not so with you. Instead, whoever wants to become great among you must be your servant, and whoever wants to be first must be your slave—just as the Son of Man did not come to be served, but to serve, and to give his life as a ransom for many" (Matt. 20:25–28).

Loosely translated, Jesus said to his disciples: "This present world system has one way of doing things; I have another. If you follow me, you will do things my way. You will be part of an entirely New World Order. My order is not made up of greed, avarice, or selfishness. I will not accept self-promotion, power struggles, or political maneuvering. Manipulation and pushing and shoving will not be allowed. Instead, you will be part of an order characterized by selflessness, service to others, and humility. Brokenness, sacrifice, and surrender will be the norms. Submissiveness and servanthood will be the methods. You will be a whole new brand of leaders. You will be servant leaders."

The disciples' selfish ambition, highlighted by the greedy request of James and John, compelled Jesus to speak about his New World Order. The entire lecture about servant leadership was born from the pangs of his disciples' avarice. James and John wanted a good cabinet post in Jesus' earthly kingdom, so they convinced their mother to ask Jesus for the favor that would elevate the stature of her boys. Upon hearing about the incident, the other disciples were indignant, not at what had happened, but that none had thought of it first. Jesus told them they were missing the point. He told them they did not understand what they asked. They still operated under an old world order and needed to shift their thinking. He told them they should begin operating under his New World Order, a whole new way of doing things.

~

Follow the Leader

When James and John made their request of Jesus, the first question the Lord asked them was if they could and would follow him wherever he went. Jesus explained to them that to follow him meant becoming a servant. If you decide really to follow Jesus, understand what it means and know where it will ultimately lead you. You've been shown that following Jesus will lead you to suffering. Jesus was referring to his suffering when he asked James and John, "Can you drink the cup I am going to drink?" His cup was the cup of suffering and agony on the cross. It was the same cup he prayed over in the Garden of Gethsemane saying, "Father, if it be possible, let this cup pass from me: nevertheless not as I will, but as thou *wilt*" (Matt. 26:39 KJV).

When you follow Jesus, don't be surprised when the road he takes you down leads ultimately to a cross, where you will have to lay down your life and die to self through the process of suffering. "In fact, everyone who wants to live a godly life in Christ Jesus will be persecuted" (2 Tim. 3:12).

When you step in line to follow Jesus, you will inevitably suffer. If you never experience criticism and persecution as a Christian, you are probably living a life of compromise. Suffering and persecution may come in various forms: ridicule, rejection, isolation, taunting, loss of job. You could lose out on promotions because you won't compromise standards and convictions. You will be criticized, and you will be misunderstood.

You may be the only Christian in your classroom or office. You find yourself being the butt of jokes and laughed at because of your holy life and moral convictions. Your children may suffer and be teased by other children because you are wise enough not to allow your children to be exposed to the immoral propaganda of public school sex education. You may be the only salesperson refusing to lie and cheat to get ahead; your supervisor may threaten to fire you if you don't bow to dishonest demands. You may be the only teacher in your building who is refusing to buy in on the NEA's liberal social agenda; other teachers will isolate and taunt you. When you follow Jesus, you will be the target of the world, and you will suffer because of it:

> "If the world hates you, keep in mind that it hated me first. If you belonged to the world, it would love you as its own. As it is, you do not belong to the world, but I have chosen you out of the world. That is why the world hates you. Remember the words I spoke to you: 'No servant is greater than his master.' If they persecuted me, they will persecute you also. If they obeyed my teaching, they will obey yours also. They will treat you this way because of my name, for they do not know the One who sent me" (John 15:18–21).

The cup Jesus asked James and John if they could drink from is also a cup of sacrifice. Following Jesus leads to a cross. You have to open up your hands, release everything you are holding, and allow your hands to be nailed to the cross. Only empty hands can be nailed to the cross. You can't carry anything to the cross with you.

Only empty hands can be nailed to the cross. You can't carry anything to the cross with you.

Sacrifice may mean giving your finances over to kingdom work rather than spending everything you make. Sacrifice may mean leaving a secure career to enter school or full-time ministry. Sacrifice may mean leaving America to do mission work far away. Sacrifice may mean holding your tongue and not speaking your mind in order to protect the unity and harmony of Christ's body. Sacrifice may mean leaving the fellowship of your Sunday school class in order to teach or serve in another area.

In some places in the world today, people walk all day on Saturday and sleep under an open sky with a single blanket, simply to be able to sit all day on a rough-hewn, plank bench and worship God and listen to his Word preached under a blazing hot sun. Then, on Monday, they walk all day to get back home. The entire time they praise God for giving them the opportunity to know and worship him. Meanwhile, in America, many Christians whine if they have to park too far away from the church. They gripe if the coffee is cold. They grumble if the chairs are too hard. They growl if the auditorium is too full. They complain if the Sunday school room is too hot or too cold. Our ability to express discontent comes so easily because we hardly know what sacrifice means.

~

The Simplicity of Servanthood

Following Jesus is great because he will lead you to service. When you follow Jesus, he will not lead you to power and popularity. He will lead you to a life of humble service to others. Following Jesus may not lead to the "head table." Following Jesus will inevitably lead to a basin of water and a towel. Try following Jesus just for one day. Search for new ways to follow Jesus. If you are ready and willing, Jesus will lead you into simple acts of kindness and service to other people.

There are a million ways to follow Jesus in service to others. You can help an elderly person through the parking lot. You can help a stranded motorist. You can offer to take your neighbor's children to church with you. You can take a friend or even a stranger to lunch. You can mow your neighbor's lawn. Service in the name of Christ will not always be grandiose, flamboyant, and extravagant. Jesus will lead you to serve in ways that no one notices or never earns you a platform of fame. They will be plain, everyday acts of thoughtfulness and kindness.

Following Jesus will lead you to simplicity. Service doesn't have to be grandiose to be legitimate. While Christ certainly had a public ministry of preaching, teaching, healing the sick, casting out demons, and even raising the dead, he also had a simple ministry of spending time with friends, holding little children on his lap, and eating dinner at the home of an unbeliever. Jesus offers a variety of viable ministries he is calling you to do: "And if anyone gives a cup of cold water to one of these little ones because he is my disciple, I tell you the truth, he will certainly not lose his reward" (Matt. 10:42).

Some time back, our next door neighbor called and asked for my daughter, Katie. My neighbor was in a bind and needed to leave her house for a meeting, and her husband was late arriving home from work. She needed my teenage daughter to come watch her children for thirty minutes or so. Well, Katie had strep throat and could not go. My wife, Kathy, called her back and volunteered to come next door and watch her children. That simple act was a legitimate ministry of helping someone in need.

Ministry may be as simple as being courteous and allowing somebody the space in front of you in line. Ministry can be as polite as baking a meal for a sick neighbor. Ministry can be as easy as holding a door for an elderly person or dropping a note of encouragement to someone facing a crisis. Ministry is waiting all around you in as many simple activities as you can discover. You will run out of energy before God runs out of ministries:

> "When the Son of Man comes in his glory, and all the angels with him, he will sit on his throne in heavenly glory. All the nations will be gathered before him, and he will separate the people one from another as a shepherd separates the sheep from the goats. He will put the sheep on his right and the goats on his left.

> "Then the King will say to those on his right, 'Come, you who are blessed by my Father; take your inheritance, the kingdom prepared for you since the creation of the world. For I was hungry and you gave me something to eat, I was thirsty and you gave me something to drink, I was a stranger and you invited me in, I needed clothes and you clothed me, I was sick and you looked after me, I was in prison and you came to visit me.'

> "Then the righteous will answer him, 'Lord, when did we see you hungry and feed you, or thirsty and give you something to drink? When did we see you a stranger and invite you in, or needing clothes and clothe you? When did we see you sick or in prison and go to visit you?'

"The King will reply, 'I tell you the truth, whatever you did for one of the least of these brothers of mine, you did for me'" (Matt. 25:31–40).

If you follow Jesus day by day, most of your ministry will be very simple. In fact, your whole life will be increasingly simple. Jesus' life was not cluttered with "stuff." He never lived in a frantic rush. His life was never complicated with anxiety and stress. Much of our stress and fatigue comes from following the typical worldly pattern of managing life. We fill our lives with stuff, thinking more stuff will make us happy. All the stuff does is make our lives more complicated and stressful. Following Christ allows you to put away those extravagances in life that add to your stress burden. Following Christ allows you to simplify and relax.

Eventually, James and John both drank from the same cup of Jesus Christ. Their original plans of grandiosity passed away, and they faithfully followed their Savior into servanthood. Their flamboyant dreams faded. Their original aspirations of notoriety and fame were never realized. Their lives as Christ's servants led to simplicity, sacrifice, suffering, and shame. James became the first Christian martyr. John's long life ended with his wasting away in obscurity as a condemned exile on the island of Patmos. The path Jesus led them down was a very different road than the two had originally imagined when they asked Christ to sit on either side of his throne. If you choose to follow Christ because you have grandiose dreams of "making it big" in religion, you are following the wrong Jesus.

Following in Faith

The leaders in Christ's New World Order will be men and women who are servants first. They place all their faith in Jesus. Servant leaders follow Christ into a life of suffering, service, sacrifice, and simplicity because they trust him. Servant leaders trust in Christ's provisions. They believe Christ will care for them. They give themselves sacrificially because their confidence is in Christ, not in the material world. Servant leaders have faith in Christ's plan. They follow Christ wherever he goes because they have confidence in his leadership of their lives. They have discovered that Christ runs their lives better than they do.

Servant leaders have faith in Christ's promotion too. They understand that God promotes and exalts them in his own perfect time. Accordingly, they are not opportunists or self-promoters. They simply serve God and trust him for the exaltation, promotion, and expansion of their ministry and lives.

Calvin Miller, Christian author and seminary educator, stated, "The number one quality that must mark tomorrow's leaders is servanthood."[11] If you ever intend to be a servant leader, you must make the sacrifices and live with simplicity the way real servant leaders do. If you are a department director in the Sunday school, look for ways to sacrifice for the classes. If you are a Bible study leader, think of simple ministries that will transform the Word of God into the activity of the Holy Spirit. If you are a group captain in the choir, take suggestions from the group members if they have a better, easier way of making the music full of praise, worship, and evangelism. If you are headed for full-time ministry, search for ways to simplify, so that when you begin your ministry you are not burdened with worldly extravagances. If you lead your household, face your spouse and children with a servant's heart. If you are a leader in any variety, form, distinction, or recognition, lead those who follow you the same way Christ did. Be a servant leader.

Chapter 31

Living Life by
the Servant Principle

～～～

T he Servant Principle has never been easy to learn. Jesus Christ, the original and greatest teacher of the Servant Principle, had to provide the greatest object lesson in history by washing his disciples' feet in order to teach it to them. You have to put aside years of worldly teachings when it comes to living your life by the Servant Principle. You have to put the interests of everyone else before your own. You have to serve the people who have stolen from you, lied to you, hurt you, wronged you. You will have to bury old conflicts, resolve current disputes, and forgive future offenses before they happen. You will have to continue serving friends, family, coworkers, supervisors, neighbors, and even strangers, despite ongoing and increasing persecution, defamation, and ridicule for your faith in Christ.

Living your life as a servant of Jesus Christ will likely come at a great expense. The moment you make the decision and veer from the worldly path of promotion and prosperity, you begin paying the price. You will see peers who don't work as hard as you get promotions you deserve. You will see coworkers get breaks and perks you do not receive. You will see people you know elevated into the limelight for the world to applaud, while you stay behind in the shadows, performing the custodial duties that must be done but nobody recognizes. You may die in obscurity, having spent so much time behind the scenes that everybody has learned to take your service for granted. When your time on earth is done, the world may reflect upon your contributions and lament, "What a waste of greatness."

Despite the world's misunderstanding, the same obscurity in which you toil will be your forum for greatness. By your example of servanthood, you will best emulate your Savior, Jesus Christ. By your ceaseless effort in the face of thankless indignation, you will lead others to their Lord. By your willingness to perform the most difficult, least popular chores, you will demonstrate to others what it means to serve for the sake of Christ. By your ability to sacrifice your own plans, your own time, your own finances, you will teach the Servant Principle to fellow Christians in your home, your church, your community, and your world.

Perhaps the simplest way to live the Servant Principle is to start simply. Look for the little responsibilities God is handing to you so you may demonstrate your ability to take on larger responsibilities. Look around your home for the small tasks nobody likes to do. Empty the trash. Dust the furniture. Scour the toilets. Vacuum the rugs. Wash the windows. Scrub the tub. Mop the linoleum. Water the plants. Make the bed. Organize your closets. Mow the lawn. Trim the bushes. Rake the leaves. Sweep the porch. Polish the car. Prepare the meals. Fill the dishwasher. Empty the dishwasher. Do the things that need to be done.

When you've finished, let your reward be the completion of an undesirable task. Offer it to God, and let his reward be sufficient. Don't be compelled to share with others how hard you worked. When others compliment you, reply with a humble, heartfelt "thank you," and be on your way to the next task that awaits.

As you proceed, you will discover that God is using the small responsibilities to train you for larger ones in your community and church. You will see that the skill you used in organizing your pantry at home is applicable to organizing the shelves of your church's food pantry ministry. You will see that you can use the same skills acquired in maintaining your own lawn in grooming your church's flower gardens and other greenery. You will see that the same talent you possess for gabbing with your neighbor while repairing your shared fence can be applied to your church's weekly visitation ministry. You will serve, and serve, and serve; and you will discover God will never run out of ways to use you for his glory.

The more you serve, the more others will follow. In your home, you provide the example. If your most vigorous activity once you get home from work is getting up from the couch to find the remote, your family will follow that example. If you are married, your spouse and children are more likely to get involved in servanthood if they see the example in you. They are more likely to get involved when they see the changes it makes in your life and the lives of others. When you serve in your church and community, you can make a difference people will see. By becoming a servant for Jesus Christ, you are living your life so that those around you will be confronted with the truth of Christ, providing them the opportunity to choose or reject Jesus Christ as Savior.

By living according to the Servant Principle, you will grow into your role of servant leader. Through servanthood, you will empty yourself of selfish ambition and opportunism to make room for humility and kingdom work. You will trust God with your future, your career, and your ministry. You will not market, maneuver, or manipulate yourself. You will take your hands off your life and simply entrust it to God. You will humble yourself before him and walk in obedience with him today, leaving whatever happens tomorrow up to him.

Servanthood will allow you to stop being concerned with positions and titles. You will become much more result-oriented. Rather than organizing recruits from an office, you will be walking the streets with them. You will understand that Christ will take you all the way to the cross in service to him, and you will willingly follow. You will give up your rights to boss others around and be in command. While you will have opportunities to lead, you will forever be in service to those who follow you for the kingdom of God.

You will be able to serve even those who follow you, because giving orders will be far less important than meeting needs. Daily, you will need to answer the question, "What did I do today in the way of taking up the towel and basin of Jesus and washing someone's feet?" You will reflect on what you did in simple, humble service just to help someone and meet a basic need in his or her life. Furthermore, you will never be satisfied with your answer. For every way of service you know you fulfilled, you will see many more in which you did not. Service to others will consume you, and it will become your passion.

As a servant leader, you will understand that there are more needs than servants. You learn the principle of delegation and shared responsibility to allow your servant force to be most efficient and effective. You will not be selfish with your leadership. Your ministry of servanthood will be like that of the first Christian churches. You will equip others to do other tasks that need to be done, so you can do the tasks God has set specifically before you.

Regardless of whether you are a mom on overload, a single working parent, a successful business executive, or a busy pastor or staff member, you will learn to delegate responsibilities for the sake of servanthood. You will learn how to delegate and trust people to do some of what you have been trying to do. God never expects you to do everything, but God may be building you up to allow you to empower others to do what you cannot. The sooner you admit you cannot do everything, the more successful your ministry can become. You may have to learn the difficult way that some things would be done better if you did not try to do them, by allowing others the privilege of serving alongside you and sharing your responsibilities and authority.

The truth of the Servant Principle is very simple. The key characteristic of the next generation of leaders is servanthood. The key hindrance in life preventing you from being a servant leader will be selfishness. If you have a genuine desire to serve your Lord as a leader of people, you must serve.

The key characteristic of the next generation of leaders is servanthood.

Servanthood will be difficult but not impossible. You can see the Servant Principle lived out in the lives of Christ's first disciples. The men who were so concerned about establishing themselves in Christ's political hierarchy that they ignored layers of stinking animal dung caked on their feet were the same men who all died horribly for the sake of Jesus Christ and considered themselves blessed for the opportunity to do so. In the time between their infighting and their martyrdom, they learned the lesson Jesus Christ was teaching them. They went out in his name and taught, fed, healed, preached, and led. They served. Untold numbers of strangers professed their faith in Jesus Christ because of the living witness of Christ's first disciples. They lived their lives to take the gospel of Jesus Christ to the world. When all they had left to give was the very life that sustained them, they did so willingly. And in dying for their Savior, more people flocked to him.

Only Christ could transform the group of self-centered men into the unified team of servants working in slavery to serve humanity until they expired their last breath of life. That same Christ Jesus will transform you as well. Jesus Christ will make servanthood a priority in your prayers, thoughts, and deeds. Jesus Christ will open your eyes and reveal where you need to quit focusing on yourself and begin focusing on others. Jesus Christ will lead and you will follow and others will follow you.

Go and serve the world for the sake of Jesus Christ.

It's all a matter of principle . . . the Servant Principle.

Endnotes

ᔋᔋᔋ

1. Stuart Briscoe, *Bound for Glory: Philippians—Paul's Letter from Prison* (Glendale, CA: G/L Books), 68.

2. *SBC Life*, vol. 4, number 7 (May 1996), 2.

3. J. M. Carroll and Ross L. Range, *The Trail of Blood* (Lexington, KY.: Ashland Avenue Baptist Church, 1931), 13.

4. Nina Shea, *In the Lion's Den* (Nashville: Broadman & Holman, 1997), .

5. Billy Graham, *Till Armageddon* (Minneapolis: Grason, 1981), 94–96.

6. Ibid., 99–200.

7. Ibid., 89.

8. John Kramp, *Out of Their Faces And Into Their Shoes* (Nashville: Broadman & Holman, 1995), 1.

9. John C. Maxwell, *Developing the Leader Within You* (Nashville: Thomas Nelson, 1993), 1.

10. Ibid., 2.

11. Gene C. Wilkes, *Jesus on Leadership* (Nashville: Lifeway Press, 1996), 12.